Philip Ray has been writing as a journalist since the 1950s but this is his first full-length book. He has written for virtually every type of newspaper and magazine from national dailies to trade monthlies. Latterly he has specialized in writing about the travel and airline industries.

The inspiration for *Animal Antics* goes back to his stint on *Travel News* where he and a colleague started collecting offbeat stories about animals from newspapers and other sources with the aim of eventually assembling an anthology in book form.

Philip Ray lives in Lewes, Sussex.

ANIMAL ANTICS

Philip Ray

Warner

A *Warner* Book

First published in Great Britain in 1992
by Warner Books

Illustrations by Leonie Shearing

A CIP catalogue record for this book
is available from the British Library.

ISBN 0 7515 0033 X

Typeset in Souvenir by Leaper & Gard Ltd, Bristol
Printed and bound in Great Britain by
Richard Clay Ltd, Bungay

Warner Books
A Division of
Little, Brown and Company (UK) Limited
165 Great Dover Street
London SE1 4YA

CONTENTS

ACKNOWLEDGEMENTS

This book owes its genesis to my misspent youth on the editorial staff of *Travel News* (now known to its friends as *Travel Weekly*) in the 1970s. One of our daily tasks in the newsroom was to monitor the national newspapers to see what frantically important stories about the travel industry we ought to be following up (those we had missed, in other words).

My colleague Tony Mertz, however, allowed his attention to be distracted by the more frivolous items and he started pinning up headlines like 'SHEEP IN WALES NOT SO STUPID' or 'MP ACCUSES PENGUINS OF BIAS TO LEFT' on the office notice-board. The rest of the *Travel News* team joined in the spirit of the thing and contributed to the Mertz archives, which eventually departed with him when he moved on to higher things.

Meanwhile, I continued to amass my own collection of

animal anecdotes until I reached the stage in 1991 when I was able to submit the synopsis of this book to Warner. It was then that Tony miraculously rediscovered his own anthology which had been gathering dust for some fifteen years and he has most generously allowed me to draw on it freely.

Apart from Tony Mertz, I also owe a debt of thanks to a team of dedicated monitors, including John Bird, May Lisbeth Eliassen, Gwenyth Errey, Jeff Mills, Perrott Phillips, Henry Riddiford, Rosalind Rutherford and Louise Waylett.

Last but certainly not least, my thanks to Alice Wood, my senior editor at Warner, for her encouragement and to my illustrator, Leonie Shearing, who gave up her Christmas holiday to take part enthusiastically in this project.

INTRODUCTION

I must have been about eight years old when I started to be interested in abbreviations like RSPCA and NSPCC. And, I wondered, why was it that there should be a *Royal* Society for the Prevention of Cruelty to Animals but only a *National* Society for the Prevention of Cruelty to Children?

It dawned on me as I got older that the British have always been more concerned about animals than children – indeed, legislation outlawing cruelty to animals came on the statute book forty years before there was any comparable protection for children. I believe it is also a fact that the best-supported appeals for charity are those which involve animals rather than, say, the disabled or elderly.

But, as this slim volume demonstrates, an obsession with animals is by no means a British phenomenon.

Readers who persevere beyond this introduction will discover, for instance, the pampered dogs of Japan who have their own fashion boutiques and £5,000-a-plot cemeteries, the cat who was nominated as the Democratic candidate for the White House, the drug-sniffing German pig who became a civil servant and many more.

In Scandinavia, too, they are just as daft about animals as the Brits. In Norway the sad story of Jokko, the noisy parrot who was the subject of a court injunction, attracted as much newspaper publicity as, say, the resignation of Margaret Thatcher or the release of Terry Waite did in Britain.

The Finns have also got their priorities right. The Swedish Tourist Board undertook a very serious study in 1991 during which it questioned 2,000 Finnish motoring tourists visiting northern Sweden on their likes and dislikes about the country. Top of the list of positive points was the cheap cat food in Sweden.

Those of us who work in the media must be partly to blame for the public's fascination with the more offbeat doings of animals. It may be a rather self-indulgent form of journalism but it is, after all, more fun to write about, say, goats who hijack an ice-cream van or rooks who learn how to plug a drain-hole than it is to cover a civil war in Beirut or Yugoslavia. And what would an edition of Esther Rantzen's *That's Life* be without its quota of dogs who can understand Einstein's theory of relativity or, at the very least, count up to ten?

In general, I have not included stories about animals who perform remarkable feats in the normal course of events like, say, the humble house martin that finds its way back to our roof every spring after a round-trip flight of 10,000 miles or the migrating salmon which homes in unerringly on the river where it was born. Most of the anecdotes involve the interaction of the animals with that strangest species of all – *Homo sapiens* – because we are generally the ones that interfere with the natural order of things, often with bizarre results.

There is, for example, nothing particularly strange about the horses of Florence performing their natural bodily functions as they transport their carriage-loads of tourists through the city. It is only when the local council orders the horses to wear 'nappies' to prevent them from fouling the streets that we begin to enter the realms of the absurd.

So in this book I have not generally identified the human *dramatis personae* – partly to spare their embarrassment but mainly because the heroes are the other animals on this planet. And now it's time to let them have their say ...

It's A Dog's Life...

... particularly for the terrier who was refused bail ... the poodle at the centre of a paternity suit ... the pampered dogs of Japan ... the Mafia guard dog who died after eating spiked meatballs ... the dog with the Abbey National account ... the golden retriever with a guilt complex ... and the Welsh sheepdog who refused to work in England.

FEATHERBEDDED FROLICS

Quarantine rules being what they are, it's always a problem deciding what to do with the dogs when one heads off for a holiday in the Mediterranean sun. Kennels are not always the most hospitable of places, but the Featherbed Country Club at Little Missenden, which opened in 1991, sounds like a more up-market solution.

The club's prospectus promises a 'complete home-from-home environment', with a well-appointed club-room, cool north-facing terrace and summer evening barbecues. Like all the best clubs, the Featherbed is fussy about the members it accepts and all dogs have to go through a strict vetting (*sic*) procedure before they are admitted. Club staff capture the dog's holiday on a video cassette which, with added voice-over commentary and

5

mood music, is given to the owner at the end of the stay.

As the owner of the club explained: 'We capture them fooling about in the courtyard, snoozing in the clubroom, chasing around the parkland, romping on the terrace and tucking into their grub.'

REMANDED IN CUSTODY

A Border Lakeland terrier called Bob was refused bail by magistrates at Keighley in West Yorkshire. Unusually, though, the dog in this case was the injured party and not the accused. Bob was held in custody by the RSPCA after he was savaged by a fox while hunting. His owner denied a charge of cruelty. The RSPCA opposed Bob's application for bail and the magistrates agreed he should not be released until the case was heard.

WHEN TWO WHITES DID NOT EQUAL ONE BLACK

A pedigree white poodle bitch called Martindell Carolina (known to her friends as Caro) was at the centre of a three-day paternity case at Swansea County Court. Caro's owner, a 78-year-old woman from Kenilworth, told the court how horrified she had been when Caro gave birth to six black puppies after a 150-mile trip to Swansea to mate with another white pedigree poodle, Lentella My Way (alias Geoffrey).

She had been expecting to sell the white puppies for between £200 and £250 each, but the black substitutes sadly raised only £45, so the £100 stud fee which she had paid proved to be a rather unprofitable investment. She sued Lentella's owner, a hairdresser, for up to £5,000 damages for loss of the bitch's reputation and 'inconvenience, disappointment and stress'.

According to expert evidence presented by a senior lecturer in animal genetics at Newcastle University, it was virtually impossible for two white standard poodles to produce black puppies – in fact, the odds were 9,840,000:1 against. But a Swansea poodle-clipper who delivered Geoffrey to the mating session rejected suggestions that a black poodle called Son of a Gun, a former Cruft's winner, could have been the father.

The judge finally came down on Caro's side and awarded her owner £891 damages and costs. Geoffrey had been advertised as 'an outstanding white male of great presence', the judge noted. 'But the canine princess from Warwickshire was introduced to her Welsh prince and she did not like the look of him. She snapped and snarled and the dog soon lost interest.' Later Caro was taken to an outbuilding for a further mating session at which, the judge concluded, a black or blue poodle must have been substituted.

The judge discounted suggestions that another poodle had mated with Caro at her home. Caro was protected in her run by two six foot fences and a strange dog would have had 'a lot of climbing to do to make an assignation'.

THOSE LOVABLE CANINE HYPOMANIACS

A survey which showed that the Yorkshire terrier is now Britain's most popular pedigree dog brought some sceptical comments from readers of *The Times*. 'Can it be that people are beguiled by the undoubted beauty of this little dog?' asked one correspondent. 'Unless they have owned one before, they could hardly know that it is an example of canine hypomania; so highly strung that when excited, it is incontinent; thinks it is a Rottweiler and will attack anything that moves; and is the bossiest thing on four legs.'

Another reader thought it was a blessing that Yorkshire terriers were so small, adding: 'In my experience of having them to stay, they all seem to think that house-training is something that has to be done to the house.' Another comparison of the social acceptability of different types of dog was prepared by *Harpers and Queen* magazine. Its list of 'yob dogs' included not only the predictable bull terriers, Rottweilers and Alsatians but also the corgi, which has long enjoyed royal patronage. The magazine also compiled a 'nob dogs' list of those which were 'acceptable companions for an English gentleman', including Labradors, springer spaniels, Jack Russells, mongrels, lurchers and Pekinese. Accessories for pampered dogs were also investigated by the magazine. They included sports shoes at £18.75 for four, waxed cotton coats with button-down collars at £30.50 and mahogany dog beds copied from one owned by the Rockefellers at £345 each.

WELSH RABBIT HAZARD

Jack Russells are made of stern stuff, but have an unfortunate fascination for the underworld. One such, Judy, survived for thirty-six days after being trapped down a deep rabbit hole at Builth Wells in Mid Glamorgan. She was rescued when neighbours of the dog's eleven-year-old owner heard barking and started to dig. An unabashed Judy eventually clambered out and ran home.

Another Welsh Jack Russell called Sam was trapped underground for more than two weeks at a quarry in Gwent. He was rescued by cavers who tunnelled forty feet into a mountainside after an operation costing £1,000 in which 100 tons of rocks had to be removed from the side of the quarry.

HITTING THE HIGH LIFE IN JAPAN

They reckon that the British are soppy about dogs, but how about the Japanese? There's a fashion boutique for pets in Tokyo where proud owners can buy anything from a pet bikini to a £5,000 mink coat. A well-known department store in Tokyo stocks fake Burberry raincoats for dogs, and business is reportedly brisk when the rainy season starts.

Japanese dogs have also taken to pot noodles, and shops specializing in home delivery have been doing a roaring trade. One department store in Yokohama can supply gourmet dogs with a takeaway tray of steak, ham,

sausages, cheese and white chocolate for a mere £50. But all this good living means that Japanese dogs are developing gum diseases because they are no longer chewing enough bones to clean their teeth. Not surprisingly, they are also putting on weight, but the Japan Trimming School can lay on jogging machines and yoga classes for dogs.

When the time comes for the Japanese dog to pass on to the great kennel in the sky, a dignified pet funeral can be arranged. There are now some eighty animal cemeteries in Japan, some of them charging up to £5,000 for a small plot. Alternatively, the Pet Angel Service can drive up to the deceased's doorstep, pop the corpse in an incinerator and play a tape of a woman's voice saying 'thank you for taking care of me' or words to that effect. Owners are allowed to keep the ashes.

TUG OF LOVE PROBLEMS

A Somerset woman divorcing her husband was granted legal aid in a battle over the custody of their trusty eight-year-old mongrel Rusty. 'It is absolutely ridiculous,' said the aggrieved husband. 'I estimate it will cost about £1,000 in legal aid to decide where Rusty should live. Obviously, I can't ask him what he would prefer, but Rusty is very happy with me.'

In English law a pet is regarded as an 'asset of marriage' and has no particular significance. But in Belgium it is treated as a child and in the event of a divorce one of the partners is granted custody. In 1991 the Belgian Appeal Court overturned a divorce court ruling that gave the husband the right to take his mongrel Ben for a walk every Saturday so long as he did not come into contact with his new girlfriend's dog. The wife in the case, who had been given custody of Ben, appealed against the decision and was allowed to keep Ben to herself.

The court decided that the wife lived in a large house and the presence of a guard dog was necessary. She said after the case: 'My dog is my whole life. During our ten years of marriage it was only Ben who was faithful to me.' A spokesman for the RSPCA agreed with the Belgian interpretation of the law, commenting: 'Pets are often the innocent victims of matrimonial disputes, just like children, and should be treated in the same way. The judge should call for evidence as to who cuddled the pet more or looked after it better before deciding who should be given custody.'

THE HERO OF KUWAIT

One of the least-known hostages during the Middle East crisis in the autumn of 1990 was Biggles, a five-month-old West Highland terrier. Biggles was travelling to his owners in Malaysia on the British Airways jet which was stranded at Kuwait International Airport on the very day that Saddam Hussein's troops invaded.

Biggles was rescued from the hold of the aircraft and was looked after by the crew, who were even able to take him to Iraq when they were forced to move there. He was finally released along with other hostages and handed over to British Airways staff in Amman. An eventful two months ended with the much-travelled Biggles being repatriated to the Heathrow quarantine centre before finally catching his BA flight to Malaysia.

THE MOTHER OF ALL MISTAKES

A Nottingham couple were awarded £500 compensation because their Old English sheepdog will never be a mother. The pedigree bitch was taken to the vet for a lump to be removed, but a clerical mix-up led to the dog being given a hysterectomy instead.

ALL CREATURES GREAT AND SMALL
(WELL, NOT QUITE ALL)

When the late Malcolm Muggeridge left the Church of England in the 1980s and converted to Roman Catholicism, his regular pew at Salehurst parish church in East Sussex was immediately taken over by a twelve-stone St Bernard, Sir Galahad.

Sir Galahad's owners explained that if they left him at home while they went to church, he would 'take the house apart'. The timing of Sir Galahad's apparent religious conversion was coincidental, but at least Mr Muggeridge approved. 'I think the vicar has chosen wisely in his replacement and I appreciate his generosity,' he said. 'But it opens up some very interesting theological questions. If dogs take over the congregations, there might be pressure to ordain a dog one day.'

A fellow member of the congregation at the same time was Sophie, a dachshund puppy somewhat smaller than Sir Galahad. 'The vicar asked when I was going to stop training the dog and start coming to church again,' said Sophie's owner. 'He did not object when I suggested I might bring Sophie along. When I take Communion I just hand her over to the vicar's daughter who sits in the front pew.'

However, Salehurst's vicar did not take the hymn

about 'all creatures great and small' too literally and
decided to limit his canine congregation to Sir Galahad
and Sophie. 'We don't want to turn it into Battersea
Dogs' Home,' he said.

DOG PADDLING BAN

Dogs were banned from swimming in Greece in 1983. Owners who took a sea dip with their pets faced fines of up to £300.

A MEATBALL HE COULDN'T REFUSE

The trial of a suspected Mafia godfather in New York was enlivened by an allegation that a detective killed a Mafia guard dog with spiked meatballs so that he could plant a listening device.

Detective John Gurnee had to get past the guard dog, Duke, to plant a bugging device in a social club in New York's Little Italy, notorious as a meeting place for the Mafiosi. On his first attempt, Detective Gurnee had what he politely described as a 'confrontation' with Duke and his superior officer ordered him to make a dignified retreat.

The following night he returned with some meatballs made by his wife, spiked with tranquillizer pills. Duke ate six but remained on his feet and was still alert. On the detective's third try Duke wolfed down six more laced meatballs. He still remained on his feet but relapsed into a state of 'tail-wagging docility' and was 'far from dead' the last time Detective Gurnee saw him. 'The dog was my friend by now and he was happy to see me,' said the detective. The ultimate cause of Duke's premature death must therefore remain a mystery – as is so often the case where the Mafia is involved.

DOG ADDICTS

Dogs are adept at detecting drugs, so a special canine cadre was trained to sniff out heroin at airports in the Philippines. Unfortunately, though, they became so addicted to the drug that they lost their effectiveness and had to be put down.

CITIZEN CANINE

The American airline USAir was sued by Ari, a fifteen-year-old mongrel, for causing him to circle aimlessly round a baggage carousel while his owner vanished into thin air. Some of us spend the best years of our lives standing around airport carousels waiting for our baggage, so we know just how Ari must have felt.

Unfortunately for USAir, Ari's owner was a lawyer, who promptly filed a £35,000 demand for compensation for the temporary loss of his best friend. Lawyers are usually cautious people, but this one filed the suit in the name of the dog and the judge rejected the case on the questionable grounds that dogs were not American citizens and therefore had no right to sue.

POSTMEN'S KNOCKS

Postmen at Viborg in Denmark were sent on a course on dog psychology after sixty-five of them were bitten in one year. The lecturer had some sound advice: 'When threatened, don't smile or make big eyes, but crouch low and make chewing noises for twenty seconds.' In what used to be West Germany, they adopted a more practical approach by arming postmen with spray cans and pepper pots. All the same, more than 2,300 postmen were bitten in just one year.

POLITICAL ANIMALS

Some say the beginning of the end for the dreaded poll tax came when Margaret Thatcher resigned as Prime Minister in November 1990. But historians will probably place the date several months earlier. In June that year, a Poole man who was the first person in England to be prosecuted for non-payment of the tax said the demand notice had been eaten by his dogs and he had only been able to salvage a few chewed-up bits. The court was unsympathetic and ordered the tax to be deducted from the defendant's wages. But in retrospect we can surely agree that those dogs were making a shrewd political point.

GETTING THE ABBEY HABIT

The share flotation by the Abbey National Building Society in 1989 raised at least one unusual query. A woman investor from Eastbourne asked if she could sign the form on behalf of her poodle, who had an Abbey National account and had been sent a form. Unfortunately, it was explained, the poodle was not eligible as it had only a trustee account and its owner already had an account in her own name. There was, however, scope for confusion because the then current Sharelink booklet on share ownership showed a dog digging up a share certificate.

RAILWAY GOES TO THE DOGS

The opening day of services on the London Docklands Light Railway in 1987 was delayed by a small bull terrier which decided to investigate all the interesting new smells along the tracks running – appropriately – across the Isle of Dogs. (Perhaps it should be called the Doglands Light Railway?) Yuppies and sightseers sweltered in a crowded train until the offending animal had been located. But by that time the day had been dogged by misfortune. First the doors of the train refused to close and then the train wouldn't start. Some would say the DLR hasn't looked back since.

O'HARE OF THE DOG

Police had a problem on their hands when Korsair, a three-year-old Belgian sheepdog, escaped from a transfer cage and was last seen bounding across Runway 14 at Chicago's O'Hare Airport, the world's busiest. Korsair responded only to commands in French, so the frantic shouts by United Airlines staff went unanswered. Which only goes to show that you never know when a foreign language might come in useful.

LEGAL DIVERSION

A jury at the Old Baily was taken on a secret coach tour so that one of its members could feed his Alsatian and take it for a walk. It happened at the end of a protracted two-month trial when the jury was considering its verdict and was being sent off to be kept incommunicado in a hotel for a second night. Worried that three-year-old

Mitch would be hungry and distraught, locked up in an East London flat, the juryman explained his plight to Judge Laughland.

After consulting the lawyers in the case, the judge ordered that the jury coach should be diverted on its way to the hotel so that Mitch's owner could top up his supply of food and take him for a walk, escorted by an usher. The other jurymen and women remained on the coach, guarded by another usher.

'Sending twelve people off to take a dog for a walk does seem to be unprecedented,' said one court official. 'But I do remember some years ago a policeman being sent to a woman juror's house to feed her goldfish.'

HOUNDED BY THE TAX MAN

A client of Coutts & Co., the top people's bankers, received a letter from the bank enclosing tax papers for signature and requesting some additional information. In particular, the letter asked for 'the date of Sebastian's birth, since it is quite likely that the inspector will want to know this.'

The client advised Coutts that Sebastian's date of birth was 1 July 1988, but she wondered if she could really claim him as a dependant, given the fact that he was a basset hound. 'Oh dear,' the embarrassed banker replied. 'I had such a clear image of Sebastian as a six-year-old boy.'

NO PAWS FOR COMPLAINT

Dogs are not always welcome guests at the best hotels but there are no such inhibitions at the Glenridding

Hotel, overlooking Ullswater in the Lake District, where they are allowed to share the same bed as their master or mistress for £2.55 a night. They are encouraged to sign in and leave their paw prints in their own visitors' book, which also lists their likes and dislikes. A collie–Labrador cross called Ben listed 'swimming in lager' at the top of his list of 'likes', while a number of canine visitors unaccountably gave top gastronomic ratings to Whiskas cat food.

THERAPEUTIC TERRIERS

Pit bull terriers got a bad press in 1991 but one group of them were said to be reformed characters. A theatrical promoter, Michael Gilmore, said there were at least ten American pit bulls under threat in Britain which meant no harm to anyone. They were a troupe called Cruft's on Acid which were incarcerated by Customs at Dover on the first leg of their European tour.

'They are lovely frisky dogs,' he said. 'All of them have been through a course of therapy at the Chicago Dangerous Dog Retraining Center. Their detention means they will be missing their date at the Edinburgh Festival. Well, that is Edinburgh's loss.'

Meanwhile, the British Government's new legal sanctions against pit bulls came under fire in the USA. The dean of veterinary medicine at Tufts University of Massachusetts described the measures as 'canine racism' and recalled a 1989 ban on pit bulls entering New York City. The law also required the tattooing and registration of pit bulls already living in New York, but it was later denounced by the State Supreme Court as being discriminatory.

Dog-rights activists were satisfied by the court ruling.

After all, they pointed out, pit bulls were reported as biting fewer New Yorkers than German shepherds and mongrels and slightly ahead of chihuahuas. As a Tufts University spokesperson put it, after its Center for Animals ran a Pit Bull Workshop: 'The pit bull is over-represented among the biting animals.'

FIDO'S LONG MARCH

An Alsatian called Fido turned up at his owner's home in Spain in 1991, two years after having been put into kennels 1,000 miles away in Belgium. The owner had asked for Fido to be sent to her, but was told by the kennels that he had been given away. There was no doubt about the identification because he had a distinctive white patch above the nose. How Fido found his way remains a mystery but he doesn't appear to have been daunted by the language problem in Spain, even though he responded only to commands in French.

FIRST OF THE SOUTH COAST COMMUTERS

Lewes in Sussex is a popular place for commuters because it has a good train service to London. But in 1878 there were few regular commuters, apart from a fox terrier called Jack.

Jack spent every night at Lewes station, but when the trains started running in the morning he would jump into the guard's compartment and spend his day exploring the railways of the South-East. He seemed to have a particular liking for the line between Brighton and Horsham, now sadly no more.

In 1881 the *Illustrated Sporting and Dramatic News*

described a typical day in Jack's life: 'He arrived from Brighton by a train reaching Steyning at 10.50, where he got out for a minute, but went on by the same train to Henfield. Here he left the train and went to a public house not far from the station where a biscuit was given to him, and after a little walk he took a later train to West Grinstead where he spent the afternoon, returning to Brighton in time for the last train to Lewes.'

The railway company even had a silver-plated collar made for him with the inscription: 'I am Jack, the London Brighton and South Coast Railway dog. Please give me a drink and I will then go home to Lewes.' When the station inspector at Eastbourne died suddenly, Jack turned up by train on the day of the funeral and followed the hearse to the cemetery, paying his last respects at the graveside.

The most traumatic incident in Jack's life was in 1882 when he was crossing the line at Norwood Junction to investigate a dead bird and was struck by a train which crushed one of his front legs. He was immediately put on the next fast train to Lewes, where two vets amputated the leg just above the knee. But Jack soon got used to travelling around on three legs and resumed his commuting.

The year after his accident Jack was presented to the Prince and Princess of Wales when they visited Eastbourne and he received a silver medal to mark the occasion. When the Lewes stationmaster retired, he took Jack to live with him in the country at Mayfield and they continued to make many trips together, travelling in style in a first-class compartment. But sometimes Jack, independent to the last, would sneak off to his favourite spot in the guard's compartment.

THE ROYAL OCCASION THAT WENT WRONG

An exclusive party held in Washington DC in 1991 to mark the Queen's state visit to the USA developed into something of a punch-up. The guests were twenty-five pedigree corgis, who were invited to the exclusive Four Seasons Hotel for what was supposed to be a sedate afternoon tea party, with dainty garlic croissants, carrot bunnies and gingerbread laid out on a six-inch-high table. One hapless waiter was even enlisted to act as the official pooper-scooper.

'We don't anticipate any fighting,' said an optimistic spokesperson for the hotel. 'They are all well-behaved well-trained dogs.' But before long two of the guests Pumpkin and Jellybean, started to snarl at each other 'Pumpkin is probably upset because she's anorexic,' said a despairing lady from the Bone (*sic*) Jour Boutique which helped to organize the thrash. At this point Pumpkin went for Jellybean's throat and three other guests tried to join in. The only dog keeping herself aloof from the mayhem was Minnie, who stood on the tea table and helped herself to a third helping of carrot bunnies.

The event ended in a certain amount of chaos, with Jellybean going for Pumpkin, shrieks from the dogs twin-set-and-pearls owners and furious barking all round The Queen was not actually invited to the party but according to a Buckingham Palace spokesman, she would certainly be interested to hear all about it. 'I hope no one was bitten,' he added. 'As you know, that can cause problems.'

DISEASE DOGS THE WHITE HOUSE

The unusual disease which put President Bush into hospital for a few days in 1991 seems to have run in his family – including his springer spaniel, Millie. The President was discovered to have Graves' disease, an auto-immune condition affecting the thyroid gland which caused his irregular heartbeat. The previous year Mrs Bush was also diagnosed as having Graves' disease, while Millie was found to be suffering from a similar complaint, lupus, which can cause kidney damage.

The odds against a husband and wife – let alone their dog – both contracting the disease were put at one in three million. One suggestion was that the lead pipes and antiquated plumbing at the official Vice-Presidential residence, where the Bushes lived for eight years, might have been to blame.

There was certainly no previous evidence of auto-immune disorders being transmitted between humans and pets, but all was well that ended well because Millie responded to drugs and was last reported to be thriving.

MR FACING BOTH WAYS

A dog with a dreadlocks hair style is a somewhat unusual beast, but the rare Hungarian Puli sports a naturally corded coat which almost obscures its head. One distinguished representative of the breed is Lazlo, who is a regular swimmer in the Serpentine in London in between winning awards at Cruft's and modelling for a Pedigree Chum press advertisement.

The Puli breed dates back at least 1,000 years and is renowned in Hungary for its ability to herd sheep. Lazlo's owner said people often came up in the street to ask which end his head was – hence his pedigree name Whichendz Leading the Way. 'Actually, Hungarian Pulis are very intelligent dogs and have been proved in tests in America to understand more than seventy-five different words,' he reported.

DOGGED BY FAILURE

A golden retriever called Bruce suffered from a guilt complex after failing to scare off intruders who broke into his family's Georgian mansion in Yorkshire and made off with £8,000 in cash and jewellery. Bruce allowed the gang to shut him in a bedroom while they ransacked the house, and only then did he start to bark. Shortly after the break-in, Bruce was found to be suffering from eczema, which the vet thought could have been brought on by a feeling of guilt that he had not done more to protect the family.

'Guilt is a feasible theory,' a spokesman for the British Veterinary Association agreed. 'After the robbery he may have felt a sense of failure. He could have been thinking, "I'm ashamed. I'm a disaster." It's not an uncommon phenomenon in dogs.'

CRIME IN THE NICK

Detectives in Brixton were mystified by thefts in their own typing pool, when several items went missing from handbags. It turned out that the thief was on their own payroll – in the shape of Duke, the first guide dog to work fulltime for the Metropolitan Police.

MUSICAL STARS CALL THE TUNE

Singing dogs are apparently all the rage these days, and many seem to enjoy giving a vocal backing to tunes heard frequently on television. So in 1991 the National Canine Defence League organised a 'Paw-o-Vision' Song Contest for the most musical performance.

The league said it was looking for much the same qualities as those in the rather better known Eurovision Song Contest, particularly enthusiasm and the ability to more or less hold a tune – 'actually some of them are considerably better at that than the average Eurovision entry,' said a spokeswoman.

The most popular tunes among the dog fraternity were said to be the themes from soap operas like 'Coronation Street' or 'EastEnders', with 'Neighbours' as the most popular of all. A remarkably high number of entries used the introductory music for the BBC's Nine O'Clock News.

CATTY REMARKS COME EXPENSIVE

No self-respecting dog likes to be miaowed at, and certainly not if it's a police dog. An eighteen-year-old youth was fined £100 by York magistrates after saying 'miaow' to a police dog called Peel. He was charged with the use of 'threatening and abusive words and behaviour likely to occasion a breach of the peace'. Peel's handler, a police sergeant, said the youth was one of a group blocking a pavement and using bad language. As he told them to move on, the youth looked at him and miaowed. He considered the miaow abusive in the circumstances.

LANGUAGE PROBLEM

A Surrey farmer responded enthusiastically to an advertisement in *Farmers Weekly* offering for sale a 'good all-round working dog with power and brains suitable for large flocks'. He travelled to Wales to see the dog in action and paid £65 for him.

But the dog had been trained by a Welsh-speaking farmer and couldn't understand a word of English so he adamantly refused to work in Surrey. The farmer asked Surrey County Council's trading standards department to launch a prosecution under the Trade Descriptions Act, but the council decided to take no action.

RANK INSULT?

An official inquiry was ordered in Zambia to investigate why a mine police dog called Caesar was promoted to the rank of sergeant. The promotion angered 5,000 workers who described it as a 'direct insult to Zambian miners'. Since becoming a sergeant, Caesar had been allocated separate accommodation from the nine other mine police dogs, who were ranked as constables. He was fed on improved rations and always went on patrol with a mine policeman of the same rank.

DIGNIFIED DEPARTURE

A dog was given the full funeral rites of a human being when it died at a Buddhist monastery in Upper Burma. The local abbot decided to give the animal a proper Buddhist funeral because it was too intelligent to be treated like an ordinary dog. The body was placed in a special coffin and twelve monks, representing each year of the dog's life, recited religious verses. About 500 people attended the ceremony.

RACING UNCERTAINTIES

Racing is a routine matter for your average greyhound, but the Afghan hound is another matter, one would have thought. All the same, a race for Afghans was arranged at a stadium in Reading, although the results were somewhat unpredictable. Apart from anything else, it must have been difficult to see where they were going with all that hair.

As a spokeswoman for the sponsors put it: 'Unlike racing greyhounds, they don't always run in the right direction. Some cock their legs on the way or forget to finish. Others run the wrong way and some are diverted by a good smell. Squirrel chasing seems to be the most common kind of training.'

THE CATS THAT WALK BY THEMSELVES

... including the moggies with a high social profile ... the long-distance travellers of France ... the tom who lost his manhood ... the beneficiaries of some generous wills ... and the cat who almost stood for the White House.

UP-MARKET MOGGIES

When you read that no less an august body than the Henley Centre for Forecasting has been investigating trends in the cat population you know that the humble feline has really arrived on the social scene. The Henley Centre found that almost a quarter of British households own a cat, although, as a correspondent in *The Times* noted, nobody ever owns a cat. It is always the other way round.

The forecasters also concluded that because of 'economic and demographic' factors, the cat population will increase at more than twice the rate of dogs over the next few years. By the end of the century, in fact, Britain's cats could outnumber their deadly enemies, dogs.

The Henley Centre also pointed out that cats enjoy 'a notably higher social profile' than dogs. It found that while dog ownership is biased towards working-class households, cats are popular right across the socio-economic scale, with professional and managerial classes more likely to own cats rather than dogs.

FELINES OF THE WORLD UNITE

Racism and sexism are old hat now. A new form of discrimination – felism – has been discovered by a branch of the Civil and Public Services Association, Britain's largest public-service trade union. It put forward a resolution at the union's 1991 annual conference urging it to 'demonstrate solidarity with the earth's wild and domestic creatures' by affiliating to the Cat Protection League. The branch also called for a 'Kitty Cat Corner' in the union newspaper 'to help cat-loving CPSA members counter anti-cat propaganda'.

SUBSIDISED RATRICIDE

A Chinese village plagued by rats offered peasants a £1.50 subsidy to keep a cat, plus a 60p bonus for each litter of kittens. So far so good, but so many cats died from eating rats that had been poisoned that a ban on rat poison also had to be introduced.

DON'T CLAW US …

British cats keen to get into show business were invited to audition for a circus in Blackpool in 1991. Russian clown Yuri Kuklachev usually has his own team of trained acrobatic cats but had to leave them behind because of the quarantine regulations. So he asked for fifty British feline volunteers for his show, promising accommodation in a special 'cathouse' and a mouth-watering fee. According to the circus organizers, successful applicants would be 'mild-mannered, house-trained, hard-working, have a sense of humour and be ready for a five-month summer season'. Previous experience was said to be 'not essential'.

LES GRANDS VOYAGEURS

French cats seem to have a love of travel. A family living in central France lost their cat Gringo one December, but found him alive and well when they returned to their holiday home on the Riviera the following summer. Tiring of the cold winter, he had covered the 480 miles to sunnier climes in about a week and was looked after by neighbours who knew him as a regular summer visitor.

Another French-born cat belied his name of Gribouille (simpleton). Born in Clamecy, he was given away when only two months old to a neighbour who moved to Germany. Gribouille was soon reported missing from his new home at Reutlingen, but two years later he turned up on the doorstep of his original home in France – a journey of 620 miles.

STRAYING FROM THE STRAIGHT AND NARROW

A German woman's love of cats landed her with a £23,000 bill for damages. After losing her own cat, she adopted a stray and popped it into the Mercedes for the journey home. On the way the cat suddenly went berserk, biting and clawing her arm and causing the car to veer off the road.

It then swerved into a parked car and brought down a hot-dog stall and a fish-and-chip booth. Boiling oil splashed on to a woman selling fish and chips and a bystander fainted from shock. The cat's reaction was not reported, but it was evidently a resourceful animal and probably took the opportunity to treat itself to an unexpected fish supper.

A MATTER OF SOME GRAVITY FOR NEWTON

A tom cat called Newton with the healthy appetites of any normal male seemed rather off-colour when he returned to his home in Lewes, Sussex after his usual night out on the tiles. His owner, naturally enough, took him to the vet for a check-up and discovered that he had been expertly neutered.

'We think it was an infernal cheek,' commented Newton's aggrieved owner. 'We like our cats to lead a full and natural life. We have had Newton for seven years. He was a noted tom in the neighbourhood. He had fights and he produced litters, but he was friendly and very popular. Now all he does is eat and sleep. My suspicion is that it was an interfering cat lover who thought Newton was a stray and felt it would be better for him to be castrated to avoid increasing the cat population.'

GASTRONOMIC LEGACIES

Cats seem to feature more prominently in their owners' wills than any other species. One lady resident of West

Hampstead, for example, left £500 for 'the comfort and feeding' of her cats Moo-Moo, Boo-Boo, Ci-Ci, Cottonsox and Baba. A nice gesture, but £500 split among five hungry cats can't have gone very far.

Rather more generous was the resident of Polegate in Sussex who left the income from his £27,500 estate to be divided between his two cats Poppy and Goofy. However, while Poppy was enjoying a life of luxury after her owner's death, Goofy was apparently unaware of his inheritance and did a runner. Thankfully, though, they lived happily ever after because Goofy was cornered by an RSPCA inspector in a neighbour's garage and reunited with Poppy in the local cattery. They were last heard of enjoying three square meals a day, with tinned pilchards, rabbit and the best cuts of meat on the regular menu.

Another cat which had a contented retirement was Blackie, who was left £22,000 in trust by his owner, an eighty-year-old Sheffield woman. It enabled him to continue living in the style to which he was accustomed, with boiled fish and rabbit for lunch and sometimes salmon for tea.

REHOUSING THE HOMELESS

In 1987, Haringey Council in London was said to face debts of about £500 million and a list of 5,000 homeless people. As part of its policy of tackling 'speciesism' – discrimination by humans against animals – the council voted to spend £56,000 on a hostel for homeless cats.

DOGFIGHT IN THE COURTROOM

It is usually dogs that chase cats, but the tables were allegedly turned in an incident which led to a fiercely-fought battle at Aldershot and Farnham County Court. The aggrieved party was Sheba, a collie–Labrador cross, and the 'defendant' was Smokey, a fluffy grey cat.

Sheba's owner, who claimed £350 in veterinary fees and costs, said Smokey ambushed and savagely attacked his dog before fleeing without a scratch herself. Sheba's back paw was almost ripped off and her screams were so loud that all the neighbours came out, he told the court.

But the judge decided against Sheba after Smokey's owner denied liability. 'There is no way she could have done it,' he protested. 'She has no history of attacking dogs or of any violence and she is extremely timid and frightened of loud noises.

'I was accused of harbouring a dangerous animal. It was a joke. Cats only go for dogs if they are cornered. And they attack the eyes and face, not the back paw.' His alternative theory was that two dogs went to attack the cat and one dog accidentally bit the other. 'The cat came ambling through our back door soon afterwards and there was no sign of a fight, her fur was not ruffled and there was no blood on her.'

THE FAIRWAY THIEF

Golfers at Weston-super-Mare kept on losing their balls (so to speak) on the fifteenth green at the local course. Some 500 of them disappeared in the course of a year until the culprit was discovered. A cat called Thomas had 'liberated' the balls and taken them to his home 200 yards away.

PUSSYFOOTING IN THE WHITE HOUSE

The Democrats in the United States had some difficulty in finding a suitable candidate to challenge George Bush for the presidency in 1988. Eventually a contender was put forward who had the highest name-recall and approval rating among the American public of any of the candidates declared at that time.

It was quite a publicity coup for Morris, the feline star of a major cat food firm's TV commercials. He was reported to have received the endorsement of former Vice-President Walter Mondale and was promised the financial backing of one of America's largest companies.

Morris's candidacy was announced – in line with normal American practice – by his 'communications director', who declared in appropriately rousing tones: 'The world is going to the dogs. America needs a President with courage but one who won't pussyfoot around with issues of peace – a President who when adversity arises will always land on his feet. Morris is jumping into this candidacy with all four paws.'

The fact that Morris was associated primarily with show business was seen as no drawback because, after all, he would have been succeeding Ronald Reagan in the White House. 'Morris realizes that prejudices exist,' said his spokesman. 'But he believes that, like records, they are made to be broken.'

Moreover, it was pointed out, in 1961 John F. Kennedy became the first Roman Catholic to occupy the Oval Office and Morris simply intended to be the first feline. As things turned out, Michael Dukakis won the Democratic nomination. And we all know who won the Presidential election ...

CONTEMPT OF CAT?

A judge in Sri Lanka's Supreme Court issued a warrant for the arrest of a cat who purred too loudly. The judge was hearing an appeal when the cat wandered in and sat purring in a corner of the courtroom, so he sent a note to the registrar asking him to 'please send a bench warrant for the immediate arrest of a cat'. But by the time an attendant rushed in to make the arrest, the cat had already made a diplomatic exit.

GETTING THE FIVE-STAR TREATMENT

A luxury hotel for cats was opened in Kent in 1991, clearly with an up-market clientele in mind. The owner explained that the cats would have individual houses with bunk beds and duvets. They would also have toys to play with, and a Christmas tree was promised for the festive season. And just to pamper the pussies even more, the buildings were insulated with glass fibre and fitted with thermostatically-controlled heating.

The owner reckoned that she would break even on an average occupancy rate of thirty per cent throughout the year which, as any hotelier will tell you, is extremely good going. But the rates are rather less than the Ritz would charge – £3 a day or £5.50 if two cats from the same family don't mind sharing accommodation.

UNCOVERING THOSE MOGGIE MYSTERIES

A book entitled *How To Talk To Your Cat*, published by Carnell Ltd in 1991, should have been a best-seller, given the number of moggies in Britain. The publisher's advertising pointed out that there were nineteen different ways in which cats said 'miaow', each with its special meaning. The book also explained why cats don't like to be stared at and featured a 'Cat Talk Chart' to help owners understand their pets' facial expressions and body language.

TACKLING A FAMILIAR PROBLEM

A special organization for born-again Christian cat-lovers was set up in Britain in 1991 in an attempt to counter some of the more occult connotations associated with cats (witches' familiars and all that). A spokeswoman for the group explained that its members had become disturbed by the appearance at cat shows of stalls selling Tarot cards and other items associated with the dark arts. So the born-again group decided to set up its own stalls and distribute a carefully-chosen selection of improving evangelical literature to their fellow cat-lovers.

MEMORIES ARE NOT MADE OF THIS

A cat-lover from, appropriately, Catford in south-east London wanted to remember her beloved eighteen-year-old pet Micky after he departed this mortal coil. She entrusted Micky's remains to a local taxidermist to be stuffed and paid a £40 deposit, but eventually all she was left with after a three-year legal battle was the cat's skin pinned to a board.

A judge at Bromley County Court was told that Micky had failed to freeze properly when he was put into the taxidermist's fridge. 'The taxidermist kept saying it was difficult to preserve Micky because of his age,' said his distressed owner. 'But instead of saying he couldn't do it, he just carried on saying everything was going fine. Eventually he did offer me Micky's remains in a bucket but that was hardly the same.'

Micky's skin was finally rescued and displayed in a frame along with photographs recalling happier times. 'Although we finally have him back it's not the same at all,' said the owner. 'He has no head and his paws are missing – he could be any cat.' The judge awarded £50 compensation, which was somewhat academic because the taxidermy firm had closed down and the owner could not be traced.

DOWN ON THE FARM

... among, *inter alia*, the designer pot-bellied pigs ... the pig who won civil servant status in Germany ... the cows who joined the green-welly brigade ... the clever sheep who cracked the cattle-grid problem ... the goat who hijacked an ice-cream van ... and the horses who were ordered to wear nappies.

POT-BELLIED PROBLEMS

The designer pig started to become a cult pet both in the USA and Britain towards the end of the 1980s. The Vietnamese pot-bellied pig first came to prominence in the States, where it was frequently to be seen in the passenger seats of fast sports cars. Then the craze spread to Britain, much to the concern of the RSPCA, which was worried that the pot-bellied pig might become a yuppy symbol – a toy to go with the BMW, Filofax and Rolex watch.

The RSPCA issued its warning after a five-month old Vietnamese pig was found in a London council flat, sleeping in a tea chest with no drainage. As a spokeswoman for the society put it: 'They look gorgeous as little piglets, but people are taking on more than they

bargained for because they grow to a tremendous size.'

Another example of the species, the appropriately-named Lo Hung Tum, lived at a suburban house in Balham, south London, where she put on weight quickly and reached seven stone before coming to a premature demise through eating laburnum leaves. Lo Hung Tum's owner said she was a 'wonderful' pet. 'We even took her on holiday twice before we discovered that we were not supposed to move her around the country without a licence. But the RSPCA is right in saying that they are a responsibility, and once a month when they are on heat they get a bit stroppy.'

In between its battles over EC beef mountains and wine lakes, the UK Ministry of Agriculture also became concerned over the pot-bellied pig craze. In 1991 it issued an edict that pig-owners must keep their animals on a lead when they take them for a walk. They could also be exercised only in designated areas so that they did not come into contact with the less socially-acceptable 'commercial' pigs. Any owners in breach of the Ministry regulations risked a fine of £2,000.

STAR OF THE FIRST DIVISION

Pigs may not appear to be particularly intelligent animals, but their abilities should certainly not be under-estimated. This advice was given to an audience of farmers in 1977 by John Gadd, a top pig-feed expert with Rank Hovis McDougall, who recounted the story of a remarkable Scottish pig called McTurk whom he had once trained.

McTurk used to come indoors to sleep in front of the hearth and never defecated anywhere except in the yard. He also enjoyed a game of snout football. 'The girl in the family I worked for had bred this pig and kept it as a pet,' Mr Gadd recalled.

'All day he would follow me about my jobs. In the evening he would come in the house and for an hour or so I would give him pig nuts and press down on his bottom and say "sit". Pigs aren't great thinkers, they don't have a massive intelligence, and I suppose he took ten to twelve times longer to train than a dog. But he did it.

'He also liked to chase apples and we replaced these first with a tennis ball and then with a football and he had a high old time chasing this completely inedible bladder all over the place. He was no George Best but there are still a few First Division teams around that could have used him.'

The moral of the story, according to Mr Gadd, was

that pigs breed best and grow fattest when they are contented. As he also pointed out, the pig is very close to man because he has a very similar digestive system, he eats almost the same things we do – and, like us, he even gets ulcers. As Mr Gadd pointed out, there is a good chance that another McTurk must be lurking in some British sty. After all, at any given time, there are 800,000 sows and 50,000 boars breeding up to three litters a year – or about twelve million pigs. And they can't all be stupid.

PROTECTING THE PIGMENTATION

Castrol came up with an important new product line in 1991 – a range of suntan oils specially designed for pigs. It was not clear whether the aim was to give them an all-over tan or to protect them from a premature roasting.

THE SWEET SNIFF OF SUCCESS

Germany's most famous pig in recent years was Louise, who won status as a civil servant to mark her skill as a police agent in sniffing out drugs. Louise had a short but successful career. She was granted her civil service status in 1985, but shortly afterwards was suspended because of fears that she was bad for the police image. However, she was soon reprieved and given her job back after intervention by the Green Party (who else?) in Lower Saxony.

The following year, though, Louise finally retired to become a mother at the age of three. Theoretically she could have continued her career as a working mother, but her handler was retiring at the same time and Louise would obey nobody else. Louise was honoured at a special retirement ceremony when she was presented with a certificate by the Interior Minister for Lower Saxony.

A year or two later, the sterling work of Louise and other German drug-sniffing animals – which included dogs and foxes – was brought to the attention of no less a body than the Association of Chief Police Officers in the UK. The head of the British Customs and Excise Single Market Unit told the top coppers that he was prepared to look at every possibility in the war against drugs. Later, though, he admitted that he had some doubts as to whether pigs would prove to be an efficient method of detection. 'They're not exactly agile,' he pointed out. 'We're not sure where we would keep pigs at Heathrow, but we're working on it.'

The British Pig Association, not unnaturally, welcomed the possibility of a new career opportunity for pigs. 'Anything that increases the demand for pigs is good news,' said a spokesman for the association. 'But we very much hope that they use British and not German pigs.'

NO MORE PORCINE PONG?

There are some sweet-smelling pig sties in rural Ireland these days. A new product called Deodorise, which contains the juice of the South American yucca plant, is claimed to reduce significantly the amount of flatulence and ammonia emitted by pigs. It is claimed to give the sties an 'almost fragrant' aroma. Its inventor is now working on a research project to see if it also reduces flatulence in dogs. 'It is a serious problem for dog-lovers who live in flats,' he pointed out.

STRESS IN THE STY

Pigs appear to suffer from stress and other kinds of psychiatric problems. A long-term research project funded by the Australian Government and the pig industry found that the animals suffer stress if they are patted and hate being touched by gloved hands. They even find it stressful if the farmer approaches them wearing gloves. Another study by scientists in Czechoslovakia found that neurotic pigs produce tougher pork chops.

PANDORA'S FEATHERED FRIEND

A Sussex pig, Pandora, became firm friends with a hen called Henrietta during her pregnancy. Every day Henrietta would lay an egg near the pregnant Pandora, who would then promptly break the shell and eat its contents to keep up her strength. When seven little piglets arrived on the scene, Henrietta took on a babysitting role and covered them with her wings as best she could to keep them warm. One day Henrietta suddenly disappeared and the pigs started pining for their feathered friend. But it was just before Christmas, so one fears the worst.

DES. RES. WITH A DIFFERENCE

The most elegant and luxurious pigsty ever was designed by an eccentric squire in Yorkshire in the late nineteenth century. It was an imposing and ornate pile with Ionic columns, Egyptian-style windows and a pediment painted in blue and gold.

Sadly, the pigsty fell into disuse but in 1987 it was acquired by the Landmark Trust, which specializes in repairing unusual buildings and transforming them into holiday homes. It now has a double bedroom, a small sitting room, bathroom and kitchen – but, happily, it is still known as The Pigsty.

MAY DAY IN BAD ODOUR

A sow called May Day was evicted from her sty because of the smells which emanated from it. A teacher complained at Banbury County Court that the 'unbearable' smell deterred him from building his new three-storey house next door to May Day's quarters which she shared with her eight piglets.

Eventually May Day's owner agreed to an out-of-court settlement in which he paid £100 damages to compensate for the loss of building time – and for the beetroot and potatoes May Day ate when she escaped into her new neighbour's garden. All was well that ended well, because May Day's owners built her a new sty well out of noseshot of the teacher's house.

BIG STINK IN THE TOWN HALL

Just as the disappearance of the ravens from the Tower of London would spell doom for the capital so, according to local tradition, would the departure of a herd of thirty Cheviot goats mean disaster for Lynton in north Devon. Not that this is likely because the goats breed so prolifically that the population is usually in surplus and a cull has to be arranged – much to the anger of the local populace.

Now the problem has been solved because the island of Lundy, off the Devon coast, has been suffering from a shortage of goats. They were originally introduced to the island fifty years ago by an eccentric owner as prey for the tigers which he planned to release there. The tigers never materialized – doubtless to the relief of visitors to Lundy – but by 1991 the goat population was beginning to die out. So six of Lynton's surplus goats were exported to Lundy – and everyone was happy. Not least the Mayor of Lynton, who reported that one goat which had found its way into the town hall 'stank to high heaven'.

THE BATTLE OF THE BELCH

We are used to seeing young American visitors in London sporting huge backpacks. So it was not altogether surprising that it was an American idea to issue backpacks to cows in ten countries in 1991.

The US Government's Environmental Protection Agency gave a $70,000 grant to researchers to find out whether belching cows were responsible for contributing to global warming and the greenhouse effect. So several hundred cattle were fitted with a type of backpack connected to a gas monitor attached near the animal's mouth. Behind the experiment was a lawsuit in which the Foundation on Economic Trends was suing the US Agricultural Department for failing to monitor how much methane was released into the atmosphere by bovine belching and flatulence.

The foundation maintained that up to fifteen per cent of atmospheric methane came from cattle – although how it proposed to eradicate this wholly natural phenomenon was not clear. At all events, having devised the backpack in an attempt to beat the belch, scientists were said to be working on a device to measure the other end of the problem.

GONE WITH THE WIND

Flatulence is certainly a burning problem, as one Dutch cow will testify. She was being treated by a vet, who inserted a tube and lit a match to test the nature of the animal's flatulence. The powerful flame which shot out set fire to bales of hay before totally destroying the farm buildings. The cow was uninjured but was reported to be suffering from shock, while the vet was fined £140 for carelessness.

FRANCOPHOBIA ON THE FARM

Cows feature not infrequently in insurance claims forms, according to the Sun Alliance company. One farmer's claim, for instance, involved a cow which escaped and damaged a car. The claimant described the cow's temperament as 'idyllic – I only wish my wife and daughters were as placid'.

He went on to explain that the cow escaped by 'holding head in air and placing one hoof in front of the other in a continual and ever-increasing process', adding: 'I seriously believe that our in-calf heifers, due to hormonal changes during pregnancy, added to the fact that some of their half-sisters have been exported to France, have developed a warped sense of justice and are hell-bent on engaging in combat with French-made cars.'

JOINING THE SLOANE SET

A herd of Cornish cows joined the 'green welly' brigade in 1988. The 120 Friesians suffered from lameness because they spent half their year on concrete – a condition with which vets are not unfamiliar. The farmer explained that the real problem was keeping the cows' feet clean, adding: 'We have tried plastic bags and tough bandages but nothing works properly.'

So he approached a company in Dumfries which specializes in the green wellies normally associated with the Barbour set, Range Rovers, point-to-points and other Sloane activities. After making two prototypes the

company came up with what it called the 'hobble boot', about a foot high and made of rubber. A grateful farmer ordered 240 pairs at £13.70 each and was highly pleased with his purchase. 'I've tested them extensively and they work,' he reported. 'The cows are comfortable in them, and they keep their feet nice and clean. It's such a simple idea I'm surprised nobody thought of it before.'

Another solution to the problem of keeping cows off cold concrete also originated in the Dumfries area, where 600 animals were treated to wall-to-wall rubber carpeting in their winter quarters.

THE BULL THAT COULDN'T COPE WITH THE BULL

It was the bull that let the side down when the ninetieth birthday parade for Queen Elizabeth the Queen Mother was being planned in 1990. An Aberdeen Angus bull was scheduled to take part in the march-past on Horseguards Parade along with, among others, the Household Cavalry, the Queen's Dragoon Guards, six chickens and a pack of dachshunds.

But during training the bull was found to be incapable of reaching the Household Division's marching standard of 116 paces, each of 30 inches, to the minute. It could not even cope with the Chelsea Pensioners' rate of 90 paces to the minute and therefore suffered the ignominious fate of being driven past the Queen Mother on a trailer. The chickens, too, were unable to match up to marching requirements and were wheeled past on a handcart.

SUMMER FASHIONS FOR TRENDY COWS

Well-dressed cows are wearing a new type of sunjacket devised by a Japanese professor to protect them from the summer heat. He developed a three-piece garment made of unwoven materials like straw to cover the head, back and abdomen. According to the professor, cows produce less milk and lose their appetites when they are exposed to hot sun. The backs of black cows, for instance, are said to reach sixty degrees Celsius after twenty minutes in strong sun. The jackets can also protect cows from the rain and keep off annoying insects.

LICKING THE BALDNESS PROBLEM

A Wiltshire farmer who had been bald for twenty years found hairs sprouting again after one of his cows licked the top of his head.

FLEECING THE PUNTERS?

We all know that lambs love to gambol, so perhaps it was inevitable that someone would introduce flat-racing for sheep. The manager of a Devon theme park devoted to sheep did just that in 1991, announcing that he had been training twelve 'really fast' sheep, including Red Ram, Alderknitti and Sheargar. However, he did rule out the idea of a Grand National for sheep because his animals were better suited to jumpers than to the jumps. 'But we will have a special week of sheep racing to co-incide with Royal Ascot,' he promised. 'They should be moving really well by then.'

CHARGE OF THE WOOLLY BRIGADE

Sheep are by no means such stupid animals as we usually think. Both in South Wales and along the Baltic coast, they have mastered the problem of getting across cattle grids, put there to stop them discovering the grass which is always greener on the other side of the fence.

Their technique, as observed by a *Guardian* writer, Geoffrey Taylor, on the south coast of Sweden, is to stand at a distance, charge at the grid and at the last moment curl into a ball and roll across. When the phenomenon was reported in South Wales in the 1970s, the then Welsh Office Under-Secretary, Ted Rowlands, commented: 'We have very ingenious sheep in this area. We are up against a very sophisticated animal.'

According to Mr Rowlands, the trouble was that once the sheep escaped from their normal enclosures they joined up with stray ponies to turn areas of Wales into something like a Wild West ranch, needing massive round-ups to catch them. More than 1,000 sheep had been killed on roads in the area in the previous three years and there had been many complaints of sheep tramping through gardens. The sophisticated Welsh sheep also took only two weeks to learn how to get inside special 'sheep-proof' dustbins.

FLOCK AROUND THE CLOCK

Richard Branson, founder of the Virgin Group, has been known to get involved in the occasional publicity stunt, so it was perhaps not too surprising to find that he was the man behind a hit record called 'Baa Baa Black Sheep' in which the singer was a Welsh black sheep called Melanie.

Backing for the record was provided by a 600-strong choir of other Welsh sheep, and a little technical assistance was provided by the electronic wizards who were on hand to correct the wrong notes. Richard Branson insisted that Melanie, being Welsh, was naturally a good singer although he did admit that she didn't always sing in tune.

Melanie's musical talents were discovered by Richard's aunt among a flock of 600 sheep at her farm in Norfolk and the great man, naturally enough, took his tape recorder along to capture a few recitatives for posterity. He wasn't too worried that Melanie might have an attack of stage-fright if she was asked to appear on 'Top of the Pops'. 'She'll only have to mime,' he said. 'They all do.'

RED SHEEP IN THE SUNSET

As we all know, drugs can have some unpleasant side-effects. In the case of some Australian sheep, one genetically-engineered drug meant that they started suffering from sunburn. The drug was developed by the Commonwealth Scientific and Industrial Research Organization to save wool producers the cost of paying high wages to expert sheep shearers. The theory was that the drug would weaken the wool strands, causing the fleece to fall off of its own accord after about ten days.

It worked all right, but it left the sheep completely naked and exposed to the fierce Australian sun. Using the traditional technology of hand-shearing, there was no problem because sufficient wool was left to protect the sheep's skin. So to counter the effects of the drug a special hairnet had to be developed to provide protection against the sun's rays.

SEX STUDY AT A STANDSTILL

A graduate student at the University of California encountered problems when undertaking a study of the sexuality of sheep. As she pointed out: 'It is very difficult to look at the possibility of lesbian sheep because if you are a female sheep, what you do to solicit sex is to stand still. Maybe there is a female sheep out there really wanting another female, but there's just no way for us to know.'

RAM WITH A ROVING EYE

A farmer was not liable for the roving eye of one of his rams, according to a judge at Coventry County Court. The ram was responsible for the birth of thirty-three lambs from ewes owned by a neighbouring smallholder, who lodged a £184 claim for damages. But, dismissing the claim, the judge commented: 'He sounds a wonderful ram. I am wondering if we should inform the Guinness Book of Records.'

CRAZY MIXED-UP KIDS

Scientists at Cambridge in the mid-1980s created a 'geep' – an animal which thought it was a sheep, sweated like a goat and behaved like a ram. They produced eight 'geeps' by mixing embryos from sheep and goats and wrapping them in cells from whichever species was chosen as the surrogate mother. The first 'geep' had the sexual proclivities of a ram and he did, in fact, father several lambs. But his goat genes were shown by patches of goat hair and his sweat glands exuded the unmistakable goaty smell.

'He thinks of himself as a sheep,' said one of the scientists. 'He was born to a sheep, so perhaps his behaviour was imprinted. But he doesn't like goats and he can't mate with goats.' It proved to be a two-way exercise, because in the same series of experiments a sheep gave birth to a pure goat.

STOP ME AND BUTT ONE

A Los Angeles ice-cream salesman had his two-ton van hijacked by a goat. He was delivering to a nearby house when he saw a goat appear from nowhere, leap on the driver's seat and somehow manage to release the handbrake. The van careered down a hill and crashed into a tree and was completely wrecked. But the unperturbed goat jumped free and ran off, having apparently quite enjoyed the adventure.

GETTING THE MILITARY GOAT

Goats play an important part in the history of the Army's various Welsh regiments. Traditionally they act as mascots for both the Royal Welch Fusiliers and the Royal Welch Regiment and, indeed, the Fusiliers' current goat was at the forefront of a parliamentary lobby in 1991 to protest at the planned merger with the Cheshire Regiment.

Going back to World War I, a charge was brought against the Fusiliers' regimental goat-major alleging that he did 'prostitute the Royal Goat, being the gift of His Majesty, the Colonel-in-Chief, from his Royal Herd at

Windsor' by offering its stud services for a fee to a local goat breeder. The goat-major argued that he had acted out of consideration for the goat, and the charge was reduced from *lèse majesté* to one of disrespect for an officer. But the major was still reduced to the ranks and taken away from goats.

The mascot of the 1st Battalion the Royal Welch Regiment, of which Prince Charles is Colonel-in-Chief, is traditionally known as Gwilym Jenkins (or Taffy for short). One of the perks of the job is a ration of ten Woodbines a day to discourage worms. But the downside is that the mascot has to be castrated to avoid smell and over-friskiness.

WHEN REVENGE WAS NOT SO SWEET

A Brazilian goat called Billy took his revenge when the fifteen nanny goats on his farm were sold. He ate the twenty-four hundred-cruzeiro notes which the farmer made on the deal. But his triumph was short-lived: the farmer promptly killed Billy, slit open his stomach and found all but two of the notes. They were in sufficiently good condition to be exchanged for new ones.

ONLY THERE FOR THE BEER

Life in Romania under the late and unlamented President Ceaușescu must have been enough to drive anyone to drink. So it was not surprising to read in a Romanian newspaper of the cart-horse which became addicted to beer. The horse had become used to drinking beer by the bucket – 'not because there is a glut of it on the market but because the quality is so low that only animals would drink it', as the newspaper put it.

Alcoholism in this particular horse was characterized by constant loud neighing, kicking, biting and generally anti-social behaviour. Its owner at first tied it to a tree outside his apartment block, but it started terrorizing the neighbourhood so he moved it into the hallway where it terrorized the residents even more. Finally he moved it into his own flat, but found that a drunken horse was impossible to live with and the other tenants finally obtained a writ to evict the animal.

'Had it lived in Caligula's time it might have run successfully for a senatorial position,' the newspaper noted. 'It might even have had a chance nowadays had the Communist system maintained the senatorial jobs.'

STIRRUP TEASE

A horse was about to remove a strip-tease dancer's underwear with his teeth in a Bonn night-club when a presumably shocked customer attracted the animal's attention and rode off on him down the street.

JEKYLL AND HORSE

A five-year-old gelding called Rami who attacked a woman in Kent was said in the High Court to have a 'Jekyll and Hyde' personality. A judge held that Rami had a 'propensity to attack humans' when he was loose on the North Kent marshes, although he was well-behaved elsewhere. It proved to be an expensive personality quirk because the woman he attacked suffered severe injuries and was awarded £25,000 damages against Rami's owner.

EQUESTRIAN EXPERTISE

Two handsome black geldings, Cassius and Buster, made their stage debut at the Royal Opera House in London in 1991. They were among the extras in the fourth act of *Carmen*, which is set outside the bullring in Seville. All went well, but opera buffs with a long memory recalled the previous time that a horse had appeared on the Covent Garden stage.

It was during a rehearsal of *Götterdämmerung* conducted by a liverish Sir Thomas Beecham, who was already in a bad mood because of an indifferent performance by the orchestra. Brünnhilde's horse wandered on to the stage and decided to relieve itself. Sir Thomas turned to the orchestra and commented: 'The spectacle may be distressing, gentlemen, but that horse is a damned fine critic.'

DRESS CODE FOR HORSES – BY ORDURE

The streets of Florence in Italy are hot and crowded in the summer, so in 1990 the city fathers issued a decree ordering that all horses in the city must wear underwear to prevent the narrow streets from being fouled. The order affected nineteen horse-drawn carriages, known as *fiacchere*, which carry tourists round the city and it evoked a strong reaction among the coachmen. 'The smell of horse manure is a smell of the countryside,' said one. 'It is a romantic smell, and certainly better than the stench of car exhausts.' Another driver protested: 'Just think how ugly the horses will look wearing nappies full of *merda* as they take the tourists around the town.'

The city aldermen responsible for introducing the order explained that it was simply a hygiene measure to keep the city clean and free from smells. He denied that the horses would wear nappies, adding: 'There will simply be a piece of canvas held against the horse's hind-quarters by laces tied to the harness and sloping back towards a sack tied to the front of the carriage. The driver will periodically empty the sack into a plastic bag which, when sealed, he can drop into a rubbish bin.' This was not the first time that plans to make horses wear 'nappies' had been mooted. The subject had already been ventilated in Britain at Great Yarmouth, where councillors put forward plans to fit similar items of under-wear on the horses which take tourists along the seafront in carriages. It was obviously regarded as a very serious matter because the council debate on the proposal took thirty-six minutes, compared with only five minutes on the alleged excessive level of nitrates in the local water supply and thirteen minutes on food hygiene.

The councillor who put forward the proposal was an ardent campaigner and had raised the issue on at least four earlier occasions. 'Anyone who goes down to the seafront will see the amount of dung that is deposited by those horses,' he declared. 'When the sun comes out and dries it, all you need is an easterly wind and it ends up on the restaurant tables.' But the plan was rejected by coun-cillors after a report by the environmental health officer, who said in a written report: 'Tail docking is illegal in this country and a long tail would come into contact with the contents of the catching device, with very unpleasant consequences for passengers, operators and passers-by when the horse flicked its tail.' The carriage drivers, naturally enough, also opposed the proposal on the grounds that their horses might suffer from nappy rash.

A similar problem in Charleston (South Carolina) had a high-tech solution. As in Florence, there were protests when the carriage horses were required by a city ordinance to wear green canvas 'nappies'. But three local businessmen agreed with the carriage drivers that the nappies made their horses look ridiculous. So they supplied two-way radio systems which the drivers could use to summon a special motorized service of 'cleaners-up' who were guaranteed to be on the scene of the crime within ten minutes.

OFF THE RAILS

Passengers waiting for the 16.31 train from Plumpton in Sussex to London were taken aback, to say the least, when they saw a racehorse and jockey galloping along the platform. A five-year-old mare, Our Sedalia, was down to run at the adjoining racecourse but bolted on the way to the start, crashed through a fence and mounted the up platform.

Our Sedalia's jockey managed to get her back for the Newick Novices Hurdle but had to pull her up after one circuit. It turned out that she was quite a rail buff anyway because she was being trained next to a railway line near Guildford.

CAN YOU, CAN'T YOU CANTER?

Speeding offences are part of the staple diet for magistrates' courts all over the country, but one case heard in Richmond, Surrey was unusual because it involved a horse. The woman owner of Patrick, a 15.2-hand brown bay cob, was fined £50 for 'wilfully riding a horse at a pace greater than a hand canter' on a 300-yard stretch of Richmond Park, including a steep hill. But the case went to appeal and the conviction was quashed, allowing fourteen-year-old Patrick to canter in future without a stain on his character.

The appeal hearing involved a great deal of legal debate on the definition of a 'hand canter' and the judge called on the Environment Secretary to clear up confusion over the use of this archaic term. Prosecution counsel said a hand canter was a 'sedate modest gait'. A policeman who followed Patrick's progress on a motorcycle said he was being ridden at just under 30 mph at a 'full gallop, with all four feet off the ground at times'.

But an expert witness from the British Horse Society said that even horses running the Derby could not manage more than 30 mph. And, having examined Patrick, he said it would have been physically impossible to gallop up a steep hill in the park. 'He is like a chair with four legs set on a square instead of being elongated like a thoroughbred.' Only someone of experience could be sure whether Patrick had been moving at a canter or a gallop, particularly up a hill, said the expert. And counsel for Patrick's owner said it would have been impossible for a horse to gallop up the hill because he would have died.

CALLED TO THE BAR

Paco, a Spanish donkey, was no ass when it came to naming his poison in the village bars in Nulles. His owner was fond of both donkeys and beer, so one day he combined his interests and offered Paco a glass of beer which he knocked back in fine style.

There was no holding Paco after that. He used to go on pub crawls, helping himself to customers' drinks, and he was not fooled when the barmen started offering him beer bottles filled with water. He just spat it out. Eventually the locals bowed to the inevitable and accepted Paco as a regular freeloader who was always included when it came to buying a round of drinks – even if he didn't return the compliment.

Run Rabbit Run

(NOT TO MENTION ALL THE OTHER RODENTS)

... including the rabbits who stopped growing tails to avoid being shot ... the ferret-racing champions ... the up-market hamsters ... the Californian mouseburger ... the intruder in the White House ... and the rats who hijacked a jumbo jet.

TAIL-LESS WONDERS

Charles Darwin would have hailed this story as proof of his theory of evolution – the survival of the fittest and all that. In 1990 the Shetland Islands were plagued by an explosion of the rabbit population, which had been recovering from a myxomatosis outbreak some years earlier. So the islands' council came up with an idea to curb the population by offering a 25p bounty for every rabbit tail which the local hunters could produce. After about a year, the bounty had led to the untimely death of 11,000 rabbits but had saved acres of valuable crops from their depredations. Then, suddenly, a new mutation appeared: rabbits without any tail. So, with no tail to produce, the hunters could earn no bounty.

A marksman who had bagged more than 500 rabbits

found one day that five of the rabbits he had shot had no tail, which cut into his profits and meant that the planned increase in the bounty to 35p was no longer such a good deal.

It was not the first time the rabbits of Shetland had achieved fame. At the start of World War II, three of their number were the first British victims of German bombing, when Nazi planes attacked the flying-boat base at Sullom Voe. The incident was immortalized in the wartime song 'Run rabbit, run rabbit, run, run, run ...'

NO-DOE AREA

It was the last straw for the population of the famous Watership Down in 1982 when wire fencing was erected around 1,000 beech-tree saplings – to keep out rabbits.

COMING OFF THE PILL

The UK Government has given up its search for a contraceptive pill for wild rabbits. Experiments showed that the pill worked on stray cats but its effects did not last long enough on the prolific rabbits, which start breeding at six months and produce several litters a year.

FERRETING OUT THE WINNERS

An important new event in the international sporting calendar in 1983 was the first World Ferret-Racing Championship, held at Eye in Suffolk. The winner was the fastest over the designated course, a twenty-foot plastic irrigation pipe in the car park of the local Queen's Head pub.

The contestants were raced in pairs in a series of heats and the winner by a nose turned out to be Concorde, a twelve-inch-long charcoal-coloured cross between a ferret and a polecat, who was encouraged by his trainer urging him on from the end of the pipe by making what one onlooker described as 'furious little rabbit noises'. Concorde's hybrid breeding does raise the question of whether he was really eligible to enter but it seems that no objection was lodged with the stewards.

Another entrant was scratched at the last moment because his owner, a US Air Force officer, said his country could not afford the risk of a second defeat in the same week that it lost out in the America's Cup competition.

A different type of sporting challenge took place in Bedfordshire when one of the regulars at the Fox and Duck pub in Clifton set a world record for another remarkable achievement involving ferrets. He kept three ferrets down his trousers for five hours five minutes, to beat the world record of more than four-and-a-half hours set up at another Bedfordshire pub. The only other challenger kept two ferrets down his trousers for a paltry half-hour.

BEAVERING AWAY AT AN IMAGE PROBLEM

Beavers are often regarded as pests when they wreak havoc on woodland or build dams which flood fields. But they emerged with a much more positive image after they were enrolled by the US Government for some major environmental projects in the 1970s and 1980s.

In Wyoming a rare breed of cut-throat trout was in

danger of becoming extinct because of low water levels in the winter. The Federal Bureau of Land Management was short of cash, so it loaded some tree trunks on to the river bank for the beavers to get to work on. This they quickly did, constructing several impressive dams which held water in the pools and saved the trout.

Elsewhere in the state, cattle had eroded the river banks, killing vegetation and threatening wildlife. Once again, the beavers were conscripted and supplied with more tree trunks and rubber tyres with which they formed a series of pools and terraces to restore the habitat.

THE KEY TO LONG LIFE?

Maybe we really should count the calories. A study at Tufts University in Massachusetts showed that mice who were fed a low-calorie diet lived longer, were less prone to cancer and showed fewer signs of ageing. When their calorie intake was cut by 40 per cent they lived 29 per cent longer and most cancers and age-related problems were also reduced.

MOUSEBURGER ON THE MENU

One often wonders what goes into those hamburgers which are sold in such vast numbers all over the world. One man who was taken ill after ordering a hamburger at a restaurant in California sent an uneaten portion to the county health department for analysis. It was found to contain mouse brain, mouse liver and mouse fur. His legal action was settled out of court, but it is not recorded if he ever ate a hamburger again.

ENTER THE SUPERMOUSE

A team of scientists in American universities created the world's first genetically-engineered giant mouse in the early 1980s. They merged a special mouse gene with one that stimulates growth in rats and injected it into fertilised mouse eggs.

The resulting Supermouse – a male – grew at almost twice the rate of his 'normal' sister and ended up weighing twice as much. Sadly, though, when he was only two weeks old he was killed so that the scientists could find an explanation for this phenomenal growth.

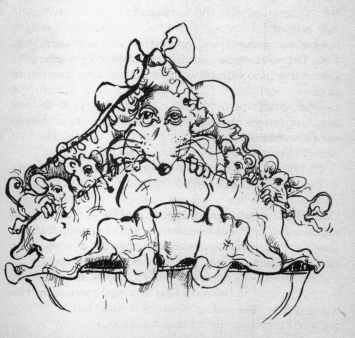

They found that the hybrid gene had prompted the production of massive amounts of growth hormone, suggesting that a similar technique could be used to produce larger cattle – or even to overcome dwarfism in humans.

UP-MARKET HAMSTERS

The humble hamster has been a popular children's pet for some time, but in 1990 a pet-food manufacturer decided that it needed to be 'repositioned' as an essential yuppie accessory. The company claimed that the hamster was the perfect pet for the affluent young executive, sleeping all day and waking when its owner eventually returned from work or the wine bar. A company spokesman commented, apparently with a straight face, that 'hamsters make devoted companions for energetic career men and women with insufficient time for a cat or dog'.

And, it was pointed out, hamsters are easy to look after, do not create allergies and are odour-free. Just to confirm that the hamster is going up-market, Harrods reported that it was selling thirty a week.

But hamsters are not always lovable, cuddly creatures. In the early 1980s, a wild hamster alert was declared in Alsace, where forty villages became infested by the animals. The hamsters, some reported to be as large as rabbits, dug up seeds and farmers were catching them by the hundred. Officials authorized the use of poisons to eradicate them.

BREATH OF FRESH AIR

A hamster called Midge emerged as the hero of the hour when a fire broke out at his home in Tilehurst, Berkshire. The family evacuated the house but Midge was left behind slumped in his cage, the once brown hamster now blackened by the acrid thick smoke.

But one of the firemen took off his breathing apparatus and gave Midge a whiff of oxygen, which worked wonders. As the chief officer reported later: 'The little chap suddenly came to life and did about sixty laps around the cage.'

INTRUDER IN THE WHITE HOUSE

The First Lady of the United States, Barbara Bush, would never miss her daily dip in the outdoor heated pool at the White House. Imagine her horror, then, when one day she saw a large rat through her goggles. 'It did not look like a Walt Disney rat, I'll tell you that,' reported Mrs Bush when she had got over the shock. 'I was out of that pool so much faster than I thought I could.' The President saved the day by drowning the rat, which is perhaps not quite in line with his vision of a 'kinder, gentler America'.

SMELLING A RAT

It doesn't fit in with their image, but rats appear to be fussy eaters – which accounts for the fact that they are not easily poisoned. Scientists at Sussex University discovered that they tend to learn what is safe to eat from a 'leader' rat in the colony.

The researchers took leader rats from several colonies and fed them on Bemax which had been flavoured either with peppermint or with almond essence. When they returned to their respective colonies they were groomed and sniffed by the other rats, who were then given a choice of either peppermint- or almond-flavoured Bemax. The rats whose leader had eaten the almond flavoured version preferred this flavour and those whose leader had eaten peppermint duly preferred peppermint.

One lesson the scientists learned was that a rat 'anointed' with the scent of a poison bait might pass on the false information that it was safe to eat. But the study also showed that rats take only small samples of a new food. So a low dose of poison might simply make them feel ill, and they would then avoid that food in future.

DISH OF THE DAY

Rats are considered a great gastronomic delicacy in northern Zambia, according to a Plymouth man who served there as a mission doctor. The only hazard in their consumption, he said in a letter to *The Times*, was that one was at risk of being bitten by a snake when digging for them in likely-looking holes.

HOLY HIJACKERS

We're used to all kinds of plausible excuses from the airlines when flights are delayed, but hijacking by rats is one of the more unusual explanations. Airlines operating out of India have been particularly affected by the problem, the country's Aviation Minister told his Parliament. Flights to London, Tokyo and New York had been delayed when rats had been discovered on board – even though aircraft were fumigated regularly and traps were laid. The Minister said one flight to Bombay from the Middle East had to return after take-off when rats were discovered on board and a new aircraft had to be laid on.

Apart from the hygienic aspects, rats endanger airline safety because they can chew through vital cables and electrical circuits. One official said most airlines would take an aircraft apart to check for damage once a rat had been discovered.

The problem in India is that some Hindus regard the rat as a holy animal because Ganesh, a much-revered elephant-headed god, is depicted as riding around on a rodent. So perhaps it is not surprising that the local rats regard it as perfectly natural to turn the tables and thumb a lift on a jumbo-jet.

ANCESTOR WORSHIP

Elsewhere in India, in northern Rajasthan, the temple of Karniji is completely devoted to rats, who are lavishly tended by the priests and feed on the best meat and milk. It is populated by tens of thousands of the creatures and they have been venerated for the past 500 years because they are believed to be not rats, but incarnations of people. The rats are said to be a completely different species from any others in the area, and their number never increases or declines.

According to legend, the goddess Karniji's son drowned in a lake, and she used supernatural powers to bring him back to life. The god of death felt that he had been cheated, so after the boy died in old age he was reincarnated as a rat, and all the animals in the temple today are said to be descended from his progeny. According to the chairman of the temple trust, the Karniji animals are no ordinary rats because they kill any outside rat which comes into the temple.

WHEN THE OWLS FAILED TO PROWL

New York City has been suffering from a plague of rats in recent years, with the estimated population reaching one rat per person. The dominant species was the

Norwegian rat, which was said to be capable of running up brick walls or chewing through sewer pipes with jaws capable of exerting pressure of 24,000lb per square inch.

The population explosion was said to coincide with the failure of a project to stop poisoning in Central Park and introduce a team of barn owls to eliminate the rats in the natural way. But the 'Owl Prowl' programme failed because all the owls' nesting boxes were immediately stolen. As the official in charge of the war against rats recounted: 'I got this call from the police commissioner saying a rat had been reported jumping into a baby carriage and asking what in the world was going on. So we started poisoning again.'

OUTSNIFFING THE SNIFFERS

The humble mongoose was enrolled by the United States in 1986 as part of its campaign against international drug smuggling. The idea came from the US Ambassador in Sri Lanka, who told the State Department in Washington that the mongoose's sniffing capabilities made it ideally suited to a new role in the worldwide anti-narcotic effort.

The ambassador suggested that the animals could replace Alsatians as sniffer dogs in countries with large Moslem populations where dogs are regarded as unclean and lowly creatures. He pointed out that the use of Alsatians at Colombo Airport had brought protests from Sri Lanka's Moslem community and added that there was little affection between the dogs and their handlers, who were 'as likely to consider a water buffalo or an elephant as being man's best friend'. The mongoose, on the other hand, was said to outsniff the Alsatians and also enjoyed the tropical weather – in contrast to the dogs, who disliked the humidity of Colombo and had to be given regular spells of rest and recuperation in the cooler hill country.

NEW IMAGE FOR GUINEA PIGS

The humble guinea pig is usually regarded as a rodent. But a recent study by US and Israeli scientists concluded that they may belong to a distinctive order of mammals which evolved up to ten million years before rats and mice.

Closely-related species tend to make similar proteins, but guinea pigs were found to have insulin quite different from that of mice, humans or any other mammal. A team from the University of Texas confirmed these findings by comparing a number of guinea pig proteins with those of other species. The scientists were ultimately persuaded that the rodent designation should be abandoned in favour of a more upmarket category.

IT'S A JUNGLE OUT THERE

... including the elephant who became a linguistic genius ... the elephant who was arrested for begging ... the crocodile who disrupted a political rally ... the rhino who became a battered husband ... the giraffes in Taiwan who turned gay ... the talking gorilla ... and the mugging monkeys of China.

LOLA'S EVENTFUL CHRISTMAS

Something went wrong with the Christmas spirit of goodwill when a five-year-old elephant called Lola turned up at the posh Cavendish Hotel in Eastbourne, pulling a sleigh, to distribute presents to the younger guests.

She snapped her reins, dumped her mahout – a local newsagent dressed as Father Christmas – dented two parked cars and charged towards the glass entrance doors of another hotel. No one was hurt and Lola calmed down enough to help Father Christmas perform his duties.

An embarrassed hotel manager said later: 'A wheel of the sleigh got caught on the kerb of a flower bed as it came round the corner and the noise spooked Lola. The sleigh broke into bits in the road and Santa fell off.' Santa commented in a masterly understatement: 'It certainly livened things up a bit.' Of course, it would never have happened if Santa had arrived on a more conventional form of transport like a reindeer.

BLOWING HIS OWN TRUMPET

A local radio station in the Soviet Union broadcast an interview with a baby elephant at a zoo in Kazakhstan. According to Tass, the elephant, named Batir, spoke nearly twenty phrases into tape recorders for zoologists. They were checking a claim by a zoo watchman that the elephant talked during the night saying: 'Batir is good, Batir is a fine fellow.'

JUMBO-SIZE PROBLEM

The New York Parks Commissioner provided the answer to a variation on the elephant joke theme: how do you move an old and irritable elephant? The animal in question was 25-year-old Tina, an ill-tempered jumbo who was offered for adoption because the zoo in New York's Central Park was being rebuilt. A safari park in California eventually agreed to have her, which gave the Commissioner his cue when he was asked what it took to move her: 'A 44 foot-long truck, 11 people to push, pull and prod, at least 35 onlookers, a very large dose of Valium, good weather and a police escort to the Lincoln Tunnel.'

TUG OF LOVE

A bull elephant charged a crowd of 1,000 people in Indonesia after his mate lost a tug-of-war competition. He escaped from his trainers and ran amok when he heard his mate's cries after she had been beaten in the competition by a team of forty local officials.

TALE OF A BROKEN HEART

Sandra, a 25-year-old circus elephant, died of a broken heart in Italy when her long-time trainer and companion left her after falling in love. He was told by his *inamorata* that he had to choose between her and the big tent, so off they disappeared into the sunset in his caravan.

The elephant promptly refused to eat and gave her last performance in Pisa, playing the piano with her trunk and dancing a waltz. Then she was too weak to go on. Specialists from Milan and Paris were flown in and tried unsuccessfully to save Sandra by intravenous feeding. She also rejected the jarful of honey which was poured down her throat.

So poor Sandra died of starvation. The two vets agreed that she chose to die because she had been abandoned by her companion after eighteen years together.

LAGER LOUTS ON THE RAMPAGE

Like soccer hooligans, elephants unfortunately find it difficult to hold their liquor. In Tanzania, for example, elephants which had been gorging fermented fruit went on drunken rampages through a game reserve. Rangers reported seeing them trumpeting, screaming, knocking

Roll out the barrel!

down trees and chasing other smaller animals. And in West Bengal, a herd of 150 drunken elephants stampeded through a village, killing five peasants and injuring twelve others after drinking liquor stored in an illicit still. The herd demolished seven concrete buildings and trampled twenty village huts during their rampage.

CALLED TO THE FLAG

Elephants in Cambodia got their call-up papers when the Government decreed a general mobilization. They went into training to help with farming and civil and military transport.

TILL DEATH US DO PART

The path of true love proved fatal for two elephants in Canton Zoo. Yilong, an amorous female, and Baibao, her 53-year-old six-ton mate, died after he rebuffed her advances and they landed on top of each other in a narrow moat.

ARRESTING INCIDENT

An elephant who was trained to beg for her master was arrested in Coimbatore, southern India, and charged by police with begging and creating traffic jams. It is not recorded whether she was found guilty.

Elephants were also blamed for causing traffic jams in Kariba, a resort town in Zimbabwe, whose residents also complained about monkeys chasing children and leopards eating pets.

SOCCER HOOLIGANS

A needle soccer match between the Tanzanian villages of Nzubuka and Kakoloa was called off because hooligans in the shape of two elephants stopped play. The Nzubuka team were travelling to the game in the back of a truck but the driver reported that the road was blocked by a large mother elephant and her baby. The team waited for two hours to see if the elephant would let them pass but eventually gave up and turned back home. It is not recorded if the pools panel had to meet to assess the score.

JUMBO'S JET

An elephant in Tanzania's Mikumi national park learned how to turn on a water tap to get a drink. The elephant, named Kijana, also foraged for food at houses around the park. She soon learned where food was kept when she demolished a store and broke into the kitchen.

POLITICAL ANIMAL

A crocodile disrupted a Government political rally in a Kenyan village by grabbing the local prize bull during an impassioned speech by the district officer. The villagers deserted the rally and pulled the bull's front legs as the crocodile held on to his behind.

After a tug-of-war lasting twenty minutes the crocodile gave up the unequal struggle and disappeared under the water. The meeting resumed, with the district officer making an eloquent plea to the villagers to beware of crocodiles (as if they needed any telling). The bull suffered only minor injuries.

Elsewhere in Africa, it was reported that the crocodiles on Zambia's Lake Mweru Wantipa eat thirty people a month, so a safari in that region would not appear to be advisable.

TOO BIG FOR HIS ARMY BOOTS?

Members of 206 Company, the Royal Pioneer Corps, held a passing-out parade at Dudley Zoo for their mascot, a six-foot-long Nile crocodile called Private Caesar. He had become too big to handle on parade, so the Pioneers decided to pay for his upkeep at the zoo.

A STUBBORN TRAFFIC PROBLEM

A solitary crocodile called Teimoso (Stubborn) who decided to make his home in the polluted waters of the Tiete river in São Paulo was responsible for some notable traffic jams. The main road to the airport runs along the river and drivers slowed down to spot the beast or to watch the police and firemen trying to catch him. At least it did bring in some revenue from fines imposed on drivers who parked on the river bank where he was filmed basking in the sun.

Nets, traps and a tasty bait in the form of a live duck all failed to catch the crocodile, who had ended up hundreds of miles from his normal habitat in the Brazilian jungle. One theory was that he had been thrown in by a private collector when the police began a purge to find illegally-held wild animals. At all events, an ecological group decided to nominate Teimoso as a protest candidate in the local elections. There was an honourable precedent: thirty years earlier a rhinoceros in the local zoo had won the election but was not allowed to take his seat.

CHIP OFF THE OLD CROC

The British golfer Noel Hunt played the fastest shot of his life during a tournament in what is now Zimbabwe in 1977. It was a wedge shot out of a pond in which a crocodile was snoozing gently. The tournament was played on the Elephant Hills course, a favourite grazing ground for wild animals roaming the banks of the Zambesi.

Hunt took off his shoes and socks and asked his British partner, Warren Humphries, to guard his rear with an eight iron. 'Then I blasted the sand wedge very quickly and got out of the water equally quickly,' Hunt recalled later. Commendably, his shot landed on the green and he finished the day among the leaders.

Another competitor, Sam Torrance of Scotland, said the course was one of the hardest he had played. 'The wild game don't help,' he complained. 'I encountered baboons at one hole, warthog at another and heard a rhino only a short way away in the rough.'

GETTING IN HOT WATER

Nuclear power stations are not usually regarded as being environmentally-friendly, but at least one plant in France is providing a comfortable home for the much-maligned crocodile. There are no less than nine of them luxuriating among the tropical plants which grow in the water flowing from the Pierrelatte plant's reheating system at a constant thirty-five degrees Celsius.

The conditions are said to be ideal because they are not that much different from the crocodiles' natural habitat, and there are no predators to worry about. They appear to enjoy French cuisine and get through about five kilos of meat every week.

HORMONES FOR A BATTERED HUSBAND

Dick, a twenty-year-old white rhino at the West Midlands Safari Park, was put on a course of hormone injections to help him cope with his two wives, Alice and Maggie, who chased him away when he started to make amorous advances.

'White rhinos are an endangered species, but so far

Dick has got nowhere near being a dad and has just become a battered husband,' said the park's chief warden. 'The mating season starts next month and we think we should know fairly quickly if romance is in the air. We are told that when rhinos mate, the ground really does move.'

PRICKLY CUSTOMER ON THE MOOR

If you go for a walk on Dartmoor, you're unlikely to meet the Hound of the Baskervilles, but you might just encounter a giant Himalayan porcupine. A pair escaped from a Devon zoo more than twenty years ago and were never found. In 1979 the Ministry of Agriculture set traps and captured six animals, so the original pair must have had some success in breeding, and there have been persistent sightings over the years.

The giant porcupine grows to a length of almost three feet, but it is an extremely shy vegetarian and is likely to run away from humans. It will attack only when cornered, but then it reverses at high speed into its attacker, delivering a wound more than an inch deep.

PANDA PROPAGANDA

China's cultural revolution may not have been an unqualified success but at least it was good news for pandas – or so the contemporary propaganda would have us believe. Foreign visitors to the remote province of Szechwan were told that China's pandas were living an increasingly happy life since Communist 'liberation' in 1949 because they were no longer hunted or killed.

'Pandas know they need not fear peasants or

workers,' said one guide who told his party that the animals had started to come out of the forests to wander in farm communes and villages, even entering woodcutters' cottages to warm themselves during the winter.

The stories seem to be more than just propaganda because an American zoologist returned to a nature reserve in China and found that his tent had been taken over by a female giant panda. She had apparently ignored a note on the tent which said: 'Please don't disturb any equipment.'

BEAR LEFT FOR NEW YORK

Conservation is all very well, but it was a bit much when young black bears started invading the outskirts of metropolitan New York, foraging in rubbish bins and wandering up pedestrian shopping precincts.

They were part of a population which had prospered after a conservation programme in the region. The young bears were left to roam by their mothers when they set out to find new mates. One bear was found standing on the roof of a car outside a doughnut shop, and another was caught making its way up a suburban high street in New Jersey. In another incident, it took five policemen to tranquillize a bear in a tree.

THE LABOURS OF HERCULES

A grizzly bear called Hercules, who became a star in TV commercials, was voted Scottish show business personality of the year in 1981 and also appeared in the James Bond film *Octopussy*. He hit the headlines in 1980 when, during a visit to Benbecula for another filming session, he suddenly turned his back on the cameras, jumped into the water and was last seen swimming towards an uninhabited island. Three weeks later he was found on North Uist in the Outer Hebrides and was knocked out by a tranquillizer dart and carried back to the mainland in a net slung under a helicopter. He was a rather hungry bear because he had lost twenty-two stone during his adventure.

Later his Scottish owners took Hercules to Hollywood to start a new film career but promptly ran into legal problems when they discovered that the property they had bought was too small to comply with local planning laws, even though it included a fenced pool and sauna for Hercules. At all events, Hercules' career seemed assured because he quickly had three film offers lined up, although one was ruled out by his owners because it was for a 'villain' bear.

Earlier in his career, Hercules was a popular wrestling performer at the inn near Dunblane run by his owner – himself a former Scottish wrestling champion – and used to enjoy a pint of beer with the locals. Not surprisingly, Hercules was the subject of some local controversy and one councillor told the local environmental health committee that an animal with a hangover was 'entirely unpredictable'. But another councillor retorted that the large number of dogs prowling about the area were far more dangerous than Hercules. The procurator fiscal said he had been given assurances that Hercules would be kept muzzled and on a choke chain during his performances, and he would not be exercised outside the grounds of the inn.

TOO MUCH TO BEAR

Two shocked bears at London Zoo fled when a man walked into their enclosure and bared all. It was all too much for Rusty, an eight-year-old male, and Tumble, a nine-year-old female, who rushed to their keeper's arms for safety until the streaker was led away by police. They had obviously had a sheltered upbringing.

CHINESE TAKEAWAY

Back in the days when China's borders were more closely guarded than they are today, an illegal immigrant wandered across to Hong Kong without a visa. He was an Asian brown bear cub weighing only 10lb, and he narrowly escaped being killed and served as a traditional Chinese delicacy at a leading restaurant. The restaurant was fined £180 for illegal possession of a protected species and the cub was taken into custody in a zoo.

It then took four years for Hong Kong to reach an agreement with China through the Convention on International Trade in Endangered Species for the bear's repatriation. Before being taken away to his homeland, he had grown up to a healthy fifty-five stone, eating 10lb of dog biscuits a day, not to mention large helpings of carrots and other vegetables.

JOURNEY SANS FRONTIERES

Another animal which strayed across national boundaries during the cold war was a pregnant polar bear fitted with an electronic bug. It had wandered from Alaska into the USSR after being tracked by satellites, but Soviet scientists promised that they would give a warm reception to this 'courageous traveller and transgressor of State boundaries'.

COMING OUT IN TAIWAN

Three male giraffes at a zoo in Taiwan turned gay after their female companion died. The zoo planned to import female giraffes from Africa because staff were running out of explanations for children asking awkward questions.

PIONEER PACEMAKER

Skippy, a seven-year-old kangaroo at San Francisco Zoo, was so lethargic that she was fitted with a £5,000 pacemaker in an operation said to be the first of its kind. But within ten days she had died – of a weak heart.

SUICIDE PACT?

A kangaroo leaped to his death at a zoo in northern Italy. He sprang to the top of his fence and threw himself off after his mate had escaped through a hole in the fence and fallen off a high ledge, breaking both her hind legs.

HIPPOS IN HOT WATER

Three hippos died of shock after an elephant opened a valve with its trunk and sent hot water flooding into their pool at Karlsruhe Zoo in Germany. But then hippos do seem rather accident-prone. Two young hippos used their bodies like battering rams to kill their father in a zoo in northern India in what officials described as 'an awesome battle for male supremacy'.

And a three-ton hippo called Hilda died from stress after being involved in an accident on the A303 in Hampshire. She broke free after a lorry in which she was being transported to Windsor Safari Park from her home at Longleat jack-knifed. It was to have been a romantic journey because Hilda had no children and she was going to Windsor to be paired with a handsome male.

Hilda was quite content to munch grass from the verge until she was tranquillized and a crane was used to get her into another trailer. The effect of the sedative proved to be too strong and an antidote had to be administered, but Hilda died shortly afterwards. A Long-leat official said Hilda died because of the stress and the effects of the drug.

TIMMY'S NAUGHTY WEEKEND

A healthy male gorilla called Timmy was at the centre of a legal action in the USA involving his love life. Timmy had been taken on the ration strength at Cleveland Metroparks Zoo eighteen months earlier and had become attached to a female called Kate. By all accounts, it was a platonic relationship because Kate was past child-bearing age, but according to the Californian-based group In Defense of Animals they were nevertheless very much in love.

The crunch came when a *cri de cœur* went out from the Bronx Zoo in New York, where four nubile young female gorillas were lacking male attention. Cleveland agreed to send Timmy off for a bit of rest and recuperation (as it was known by US soldiers during the Vietnam war), but it was then that the animal rights activists moved in.

The International Primate Protection League said gorillas in the wild often pined away if they were parted and they sometimes died of stress after a mate died. But a committee of experts recommended Timmy's move to New York to assist the survival of the gorilla species. They also made the point that gorillas in the wild travel great distances to find a suitable mate and said Timmy's journey to the Bronx was simply the animal equivalent of a naughty weekend in Paris.

But the activists went to court seeking an injunction to

prevent Timmy's transfer. The action was unsuccessful, the judge rejecting the legal argument over 'emotional distress' after hearing that gorillas were naturally polygamous.

QUICK-LEARNING PRIMATE

Koko, a talking gorilla, was the most unusual student in the psychology department at Stanford University in California. Koko was loaned by San Francisco Zoo to be the star in a research project aimed at 'extending our knowledge of biological heritage'.

Within a couple of years, Koko had learned 300 words and was learning new ones at the rate of between ten and fifteen a month. Her teacher said the research could lead to the development of new techniques for treating mentally-handicapped children. Koko was such a willing pupil that the possibility of her moving on to reading and mathematics was not ruled out.

LORD OF THE RINGS

The most bizarre wedding ceremony for many a long year was surely Elizabeth Taylor's eighth marriage in 1991. Apart from the happy couple, the most notable performer was a chimpanzee called Bubbles who dressed in a dinner jacket and boiled shirt to act as the ringbearer at the ceremony, held at pop singer Michael Jackson's ranch in California. Later a dozen giraffes, llamas and zebras mingled with ex-President Ronald Reagan and 200 other guests during the reception.

HIGH LIFE FOR A STOWAWAY

A chimpanzee who stowed away on a Danish cargo ship in an African port thrived on a diet of bananas and whisky during the voyage to Europe. He managed to evade capture on arrival in Hamburg by climbing a mast.

APES LOSE GRAPES

Because of soaring fruit prices, twenty chimpanzees at a zoo in Leicestershire who appeared in tea commercials on TV had to forego their daily ration of grapes and go on a regime of bread and jam.

LOVE FINDS A WAY HOME

A love-sick monkey called Jenny pined when her mate Jinxy ran away. So her Yorkshire owner taped her love calls and played them over loudspeakers outside his house to try and tempt Jinxy home. It worked, because Jinxy soon turned up in the nearby woods and the happy pair were reunited. They both lived happily ever afterwards and their relieved owner said: 'The monkeys are very romantic and cuddle up at night.'

NOT SUCH A SWEET LIFE ON THE ROCK

The well-known apes on the Rock of Gibraltar now have a much healthier, if less enjoyable, lifestyle. After getting fat and lazy over many years through a diet of chocolates and sweets fed them by tourists, they are now in a wardened park and living on a less sugary regime.

The Rock's apes are actually Barbary macaques and their history goes back at least to the times of Nelson. Since 1915 they had been on the payroll of the Army, but now come under the control of the Gibraltar Government. The director of the park said the opening of Gibraltar's frontier with Spain in 1984 was something of a disaster for the apes. More than three million people a year visited Gibraltar and many of them fed the apes the chocolates and other sweets which they like so much.

'The animals are often addicted and obese with the result that the birth rate has fallen,' he said. 'A male will leave a female on heat to get his supply of Smarties. Degraded individuals lose interest in mating and fight over food.' The apes are now being fed on food pellets, which sound rather boring but should help to fight the flab.

The health of the Gibraltar apes is a matter of some concern because, according to tradition, if they leave the Rock then so will the British. During the Great Siege of 1783, it is said, their alarm barks alerted the garrison to a Spanish attack.

CHINA'S GANG OF THREE

A few years ago a gang of three muggers turned their attention to tourists visiting the ancient Buddhist shrines of Mount Omel in China. Their leader had a harelip, his chief follower had three fingers on his right hand and the third had only one eye. The one thing they had in common was that they were all monkeys.

MONKEY BUSINESS ON SAFARI

Two travel agents on a safari trip to Kenya who decided to take a siesta one afternoon had an unwelcome visitor. One of them woke up in his room at Samburu Lodge to find an intruder systematically going through his suitcase. Grabbing his spectacles, he came face to face with a full-size baboon which, unabashed, continued unpacking the luggage.

The agent ran to the door to call for help, upon which the baboon left the room via the window through which he had come, but not before liberating a packet of strong mints and a Barclaycard.

The next port of call for the baboon was the room occupied by a young lady travel agent, who was suffering from a stomach upset and had decided to have a rest. She shouted unsuccessfully for help before the baboon finally left, discarding the strong mints and exchanging them for a packet of laxative tablets.

A spokesman for the company organizing the safari expressed concern, but said it was unwise to 'go too far to isolate the visitor from the wildlife because, in doing so, we may destroy the holiday experience.'

TARZAN'S FRIEND TAKES IT EASY

Many years after his days of stardom, Chetta the chimpanzee who appeared in the Tarzan movies with Johnny Weissmuller and Lex Barker was still enjoying his retirement at the age of fifty on a ranch near Los Angeles. He enjoyed an occasional cigar and a glass of brandy and took a stroll in the neighbourhood or a quiet drive to pass the time.

Chetta could still go through his old Tarzan routines,

standing on his head and clapping with his feet, doing somersaults and curling his top lip to give a big grin. But most of the time he just sat back on the couch of his owner and took life easy. And who could blame him after such an energetic career?

BLAST-OFF FOR A LONG LIFE

Space travel could make one live longer if American experience is any guide. Certainly one of the first American astronauts, a squirrel monkey called Baker, broke the longevity records. She was sent 300 miles into space on a Jupiter rocket in 1959 and was still around for the 25th anniversary party in 1984 – a lifespan three times as long as squirrel monkeys in captivity and twice as long as members of her species in the wild.

At a bananas-and-jelly celebration to mark the anniversary, a doctor who supervised her diet said: 'She is on her third mate – and she has outlived two of them. 'Did space flight extend her life expectancy? I don't know, but she has lived a full and remarkable life and has never had any health problems except some minor skin troubles.'

However, Baker did have a pampered lifestyle both before and after her space flight. She always had the best food available and a cage which was climate-controlled to simulate the environment of a tropical rain forest. After Baker's sub-orbital flight, in which she was strapped into a special space suit, she became a national figure in the USA, making frequent appearances on TV programmes like the Dinah Shore Show and Good Morning, America.

PUTTING CONSERVATION IN PERSPECTIVE

Anyone concerned with the balance of nature should take note of a wise observation made by a game warden in Bangladesh, as quoted by the retired Major-General A.S. Jeapes in a letter to *The Times*. The general said he had once suggested shooting a man-eating tiger that was preying on fishermen. But the warden's reaction was one of horror. 'Oh no,' he said. 'We have many fishermen but very few tigers.'

SNAKES ALIVE
(AND OTHER SLIPPERY CUSTOMERS)

... including the boa constrictor who faced a subpoena application in a New York court ... the friendly python who found a home in a Glasgow school ... the worms who became a surprise ingredient in a Quiche Lorraine ... the alarming decline in the French snail population ... and the African snails with a fatal fascination for Guinness.

STOWAWAY SERPENT

An unexpected passenger in the shape of a three-foot-long snake was found on a Philippine Airlines flight between Manila and Tokyo. It was first spotted by alarmed passengers in the economy section of the aircraft. An overhead luggage bin was slightly ajar and the snake popped its head out, had a quick look around and then started to slither across the ceiling. The cabin crew quickly managed to charm the snake back into its bin and slammed the lid shut until the aircraft landed. No one claimed the snake once the plane arrived at Tokyo's Narita Airport so it was promptly impounded.

A London spokesman for the airline said the snake had been arrested as an illegal immigrant, but he had no idea how it came to be on board in the first place. 'It sounds like something from Monty Python,' he added. And, asked how the snake came to be in the overhead bin in the first place, the spokesman replied: 'Maybe it couldn't find a seat.' An over-booked flight on Philippine Airlines? Perish the thought.

CONSTRICTED CONFESSION

A Manhattan judge was asked by a defence attorney to subpoena a seven-foot boa constrictor on the grounds that the police had used the snake as an 'instrument of terror' to secure a confession from a prisoner.

The defendant was a Taiwanese immigrant who was accused of killing three Vietnamese youths and maintained that after he was arrested two police officers forced him to sit near the snake while he was being interrogated. During the questioning, he maintained, an officer had threatened to let the snake loose on him unless he confessed to the shooting.

'Imagine the fear he felt,' said the attorney, asking the judge to experience the 'terror of the snake' and hand down a ruling that the defendant's admissions to the police were involuntary and could not be used as evidence against him. There was, said the attorney, a strong legal precedent for calling the boa constrictor as a witness. In 1908, a New York Appeals Court had overturned a decision in which a judge refused to allow into court a horse that was at issue in the case.

However, the Manhattan judge declined to grant a subpoena after hearing that the snake belonged to a policeman who had left it in the police station house because he could no longer take care of it.

BOA IN THE BATHROOM

The police in South London issued a warning that a six-foot boa constrictor, thought to be lurking in the sewers of Balham after disappearing from its owner's bathroom, could pop up in neighbouring lavatories. The police gave the profound advice that if it did appear the lavatory seat should be shut immediately.

THE BITER BITTEN

As a variation on the 'man bites dog' theme, a sixteen-foot-long python was bitten to death by a fourteen-year-old boy after it attacked him in Richmond, South Africa. The boy said the snake coiled round his legs in some long grass. After hitting it with a stick, he sank his teeth into its neck and held on. It took two men to carry the dead snake and take it to the police station.

Not so fortunate was a fifteen-year-old boy who was swallowed whole by a python which he disturbed while searching a mountain cave for bats in the Philippines. Local villagers managed to kill and slice open the snake but the youth was dead.

TOO MUCH TO SWALLOW

A ten-foot python had to undergo surgery after trying to swallow a goat in the Indian state of Gujarat. The snake panicked at the sight of advancing villagers and tore its throat while trying to regurgitate the goat. There was no news of the goat's fate.

SNAKES ALIGHT

A four-foot pine snake which swallowed two fifteen-watt light bulbs three times the size of its head underwent surgery in Gainesville, Florida to have them removed.

MISSING MONTY

A three-foot python named, inevitably, Monty had four years of freedom in a Glasgow school. He went missing after thieves broke into Cranhill Secondary School and the staff assumed he had been stolen.

But finally Monty was found hiding behind a cupboard. A biology teacher reported: 'He's obviously been living on mice, although he would be hard put to swallow one. He's quite a friendly snake, although a bit shy. There's no danger of him crushing anyone.'

POISON PROGENY

A horned viper from Gabon, one of the world's most poisonous snakes, set a world record at Madrid Zoo by producing seventy-one offspring, of which sixty-three survived.

SOCCER HOOLIGANS?

Police kept a special watch for two eight-foot pythons among the fans arriving at Southampton FC's ground for a local derby match with Portsmouth. The snakes were stolen from the home of a local herpetologist, and subsequently two pet rabbits went missing which police said could have been stolen to feed the snakes. A police spokesman observed sagely that it was unlikely anyone would be able to take the snakes into the ground without being spotted.

PYTHONS IN THE PANTS

An assistant in a Leeds pet shop noticed that one of the customers was walking out of the shop in a rather strange way. It turned out that he had stolen two live pythons almost four feet long and had stuffed them down his underpants. The man, who was fined £50 for theft, had previously exchanged two small lizards at the shop for one large one but felt he had been cheated and went back to the shop to remonstrate with the manager.

As he was leaving the shop he picked up the pythons from a tank and stuffed them down his underpants - even though he had no idea whether they would bite. One of the snakes died at his home from an infection and he gave the other one away.

THIS MORTAL COIL

A six-foot royal python was discovered coiled round a refrigerator motor in a flat which a young couple were renovating at Aix-en-Provence in France. The previous owners had apparently left the snake there. The fire brigade was called and the python was knocked out with a chemical spray before being donated to a local zoo.

TWO HEADS NOT BETTER THAN ONE

A snake with two heads and two tails was captured in the Argentinian town of Saladillo. One head ate voraciously but the other did not function at all.

A CASE OF OVERKILL?

Three highly poisonous saw-scale snakes went on duty to guard a 360-carat blue star sapphire worth $430,000 which went on display in a showcase at an exhibition of Sri Lankan gems in Stockholm. Exhibition officials said a person bitten by a saw-scale needed at least eighty millilitres of serum to survive. The snakes' poison was said to be capable of killing a person within ten minutes, although it could take up to three weeks. Just in case, a supply of serum was kept ready at a nearby hospital.

DIET OF WORMS

A gastronomic delicacy called *Quiche Lorraine avec Ver de Terre* won a $500 prize for a teacher in a cookery contest in California. The key to his success was the *ver de terre* – in other words, the common earthworm. Worms were among the ingredients in all 2,000 dishes entered in the contest organized by a fishing bait company. Worm fritters and worm butterscotch were other contenders for the top prize.

The head of the company organizing the contest commented: 'We don't think earthworms will be on everybody's table but the contest gives us the chance to tell people that worms are seventy-three per cent protein and are low in cholesterol. When you eat them plain after boiling them, they taste rather like Shredded Wheat.'

NOT-SO-ENDANGERED SPECIES

Australians were surprised when they learned that the world's longest invertebrate, the giant Gippsland earthworm, which grows to a length of nine feet, was listed by the World Wildlife Fund as an endangered species. As one naturalist commented: 'You can dig up a couple of thousand of them off one acre here.'

CHEATING IN THE CHARM SCHOOL

The annual worm-charming championship sounds a harmless enough sporting activity, but the event has been known to produce its fair share of cheating. Three teams were banned for life in 1991 after the competition organizers discovered that they had used 'dodgy substances'.

The landlord of the Devon pub where the championships were held said: 'They used things that would damage the worms. It is made clear in the rules that the worms have to be put back in their holes.' The technique of worm charming is to moisten an area of ground and for one member of the team to tap the soil. Each three-person team – a charmer, a catcher and a counter – then has fifteen minutes to extract as many worms from the soil as possible.

This particular contest was won by a Dartmouth team which charmed sixty-five worms to the surface. In the world championship event, more sophisticated techniques like tap dancing, electronic devices and a string quartet have been brought into play. They seemed to pay off because they produced a record number of 513 worms from a three-square-metre plot in half-an-hour.

WAR OF THE WORMS

Scotland has suffered from unwelcome invaders over the centuries. The latest is a voracious immigrant known as the New Zealand flatworm (or *artoposthia triangulata* to its Latin-speaking friends). The new arrival has a purple-brown upper surface and hides under garden pots. It arrived from New Zealand hidden in imported plants, but its favourite food is the indigenous earthworm. The Biological Recording in Scotland Campaign has been trying to find out how the New Zealanders deal with the pests, but in the meantime it has asked people to kill them.

SHELL-SHOCKED MARRIAGE

A snail trainer's marriage broke up after four months, and it was the snails who were to blame. After his wedding the trainer said he was giving up snails for ever. But he then signed a contract for a series of TV appearances about snails. 'That was the last straw for my wife,' he said.

POUR ENCOURAGER LES ESCARGOTS

We are all taught from birth that the French exist on a diet of frogs' legs and snails. But it was rather disconcerting to learn in the early days of President Mitterrand's regime that France was no longer self-sufficient in snails. The country was spending no less than £9 million a year on buying hundreds of millions of the succulent gastropods from abroad, mostly from Turkey and Greece.

The French Government's answer was to cut the number of Customs posts through which snails could be imported from 400 to about 100. The ostensible reason was to ensure better veterinary control, but the chairman of one snail-canning factory said the re-routeing of snails through a more distant Customs post would actually increase snail mortality.

At the same time the Government launched a programme to encourage the commercial breeding of

more snails within France. One company responded by producing a do-it-yourself snail cultivator protected by netting to keep the birds out and an electrified fence to keep the snails in. There was also a polystyrene house where the snails could huddle together on a cold night. The complete outfit cost about £300, but it was claimed that it could bring in a profit of about £100 a year.

FROM LETTUCE TO LETTERS

We thought that the Post Office had been running out of excuses for the late delivery of letters but Sir Andrew Gilchrist, a former British Ambassador to Indonesia, discovered a new one. He received a letter several weeks late, adorned with a Royal Mail sticker apologising for the fact that it had been damaged and adding the explanation 'Eaten by snails'.

'The snails had eaten right through the envelope,' Sir Andrew said later. 'I could tell it was a snail because what was left of the letter was slimy.' The letter had been handled by Salisbury Post Office, which explained: 'We get quite a few letters that have been eaten by snails, probably because they find the glue on stamps irresistible. It always gets worse on Bank Holidays because the letters are left lying around for longer.

'The trouble is that when you try to explain to people why their letters are chewed up they look at you as if you're really stupid. They think it's just another Post Office excuse.'

WHEN GUINNESS IS NOT GOOD FOR YOU

An orchid nursery in Kenya was alarmed by a plague of large African snails which devoured the blooms of its 32,000 valuable plants. Normal pesticides had no effect, but the owner of the nursery discovered that the snails had a fatal fascination for Guinness.

Fortuitously her husband was chairman of East African Breweries, which brewed Guinness under licence, so she stocked up with the delectable brew and assembled hundreds of tins containing Guinness which she placed at night along the trails through the nursery. Hundreds of snails climbed over the edges of tins to investigate the attractive smell and quickly died an alcoholic death. Some of the luckier ones managed to stagger away but always returned the following night for a hair of the dog.

Two weeks after the campaign started, the snails got through 193 bottles of Guinness and almost 1,400 had died. One would have thought that the snails had demonstrated a new niche market for Guinness. But shortly after the massacre at the nursery East African Breweries announced that it was no longer producing Guinness because sales had dropped.

TWO'S COMPANY, THREE HUNDRED'S A CROWD

A Sussex animal lover who bought two giant African land snails for 10p each made the fatal mistake of keeping them together. Love found a way as usual, and more than 300 baby snails and another 300 eggs soon appeared on the scene. A local vet who took advice from the Royal Veterinary College said he had no alternative but to boil the baby snails and eggs alive, but their owner decided to persevere with the proud parents, named Rudolph and Margot L'Escargot after two famous ballet dancers 'because of their grace'. 'I suppose I just have to spend the next eight to ten years destroying hundreds of eggs,' she said.

GETTING THEIR OATS

A thumbnail snail, almost extinct on its native Moorea in the Pacific, has produced two young at Nottingham University. They were said to be thriving on a diet of porridge oats, vitamin pills and fish food.

LONELINESS OF THE LONG-DISTANCE TURTLE

An unusual immigrant arrived on the Dingle peninsula in County Kerry in 1990. It was a young loggerhead turtle, only twelve inches long, normally found off the coast of Florida. Timmy, as he was christened, was exhausted after his long journey and was also feeling the cold in Ireland's wintry water. A Dublin businessman gave Timmy the VIP treatment. First he was flown to Dublin, then transferred to an Irish military helicopter and, with special permission, flown across the border to Northern Ireland. There he recuperated in a heated sea-water aquarium before being put on the plane back to Florida.

CONFINED TO BARRACKS

Colin, a lovesick tortoise, was confined to his cage after terrorizing customers in a Devon café. One visitor was left with a torn shoe after Colin's attentions.

LETTUCE LEGACY

A Hull woman left £26,000 to the local RSPCA branch for the 'care, upkeep and maintenance' of her 34-year-old tortoise Fred. With a life expectancy of a further eighty years, Fred could certainly look forward to a comfortable existence. As the RSPCA branch secretary commented: 'He'll have the best lettuce and cabbage leaves for the rest of his life.'

A VERY SENIOR CITIZEN

A tortoise belonging to the Earl of Devon is thought to be Britain's oldest animal. Timothy is believed to be at least 140 years old and, although sexed as a female in the 1920s, is still referred to by the Earl's family as a 'him'. Timothy is thought to have been a mascot on a Royal Navy ship, and a distant cousin is said to have given him to the Devon family when the ship was sent to Antarctica.

Timothy has had a number of adventures, including one episode when he got drunk through over-indulging in azalea blossom. His home is at the 600-year-old family seat, Powderham Castle, and the family motto 'Where have I fallen, what have I done?' is branded on his back to identify him. According to the Earl, Timothy leads a contented life, eating his way round the garden, hibernating from November to March and showing no signs of his great age.

THE CHARGE OF
THE CREEPY-CRAWLIES

... including revelations about the
cockroach as a gastronomic delicacy
... musical reflections on the plight of
the bumble bee ... the scorpion who
was an exhibit at an Old Bailey trial ...
and the sea lice who can't stand the
smell of onions.

CREATING A BEETLE BOOM

This chapter is not the longest in this book, but perhaps
it should be. While there are estimated to be only about
8,000 species of birds in the world, there are between
one and three million species of insects. Of these about
two-thirds are beetles.

So it is not surprising that when the scientist J.B.S.
Haldane was asked by theological colleagues what his
studies revealed about the nature of the Creator, he
replied: 'An inordinate fondness for beetles.'

CRUNCH IN THE CASSEROLE

Patients and nurses at a leading London teaching
hospital had an unusual gastronomic experience when

113

cockroaches turned up in the chicken casserole served up for lunch one day. One patient discharged himself and a nurse was sick for three hours after finding the unusual garnishing among the chicken pieces.

But patients were reassured by the hospital's catering manager that cockroaches in chicken stew were quite harmless if they were cooked properly. As long as they had been cooked to the correct temperature any bacteria would have been killed, he pointed out. The hospital's consultant microbiologist agreed that there was no fear of food poisoning if the cockroaches were cooked. The danger came when they dropped into food just before it was served, he said.

PLUS A BOWL OF FRIED LICE?

Take a closer look at the menu the next time you go to a Chinese restaurant. A Chinese newspaper recently gave some hints on cockroach cuisine, claiming that it was more nutritious than beef. Sample recommended dishes included fried cockroach, cockroach-studded pancakes or cockroach porridge. But for a real gastronomic experience, the newspaper recommended marinating cockroaches in wine for a day, then frying them in beef fat and smothering them in chocolate.

OLD-AGE PALS

A Nottinghamshire pet-shop owner announced plans to sell giant African cockroaches at £1.20 a pair because, he said, they were cheap to keep and made ideal company for senior citizens.

LEGLESS DESIGNER LABEL

A highlight of the fifth annual Roach-a-rama festival in New York was a faux-pearl necklace created by the noted fashion designer Karen Raus with a dead cockroach as its centrepiece. 'I knitted him a little sweater first,' she said. 'But his little legs broke off when I tried to pull them through the sleeves.'

OFF THE RAILS

An Italian railwayman went to a hospital in Naples complaining about a bad ear-ache. A doctor duly probed the ear and extracted an inch-long cockroach.

CRINGE EVENT AT THE OPERA

An unusual sport has emerged in the former USSR. An independent media company specializing in sporting events and the general director of the Kharkhov Opera in the Ukraine joined forces to mount and broadcast a series of live cockroach races in the grand foyer of the Opera House. 'We have imported two dozen racing cockroaches from the USA,' said the chairman of the media company.

'But now the bureaucrats want to stop it. It took twenty years and 25 million roubles to build the Opera House. The people who go there are all officials and visiting businessmen. The Opera is in debt and the only hope of saving it is through events like the Cockroach Ascot.'

AIR ON THE BEE STRING

The musical abilities of the bumble bee (*bombus terrestris*) came under close scrutiny on the correspondence page of *The Times*. In 1989 Dr G.B.R. Walkley wrote to the newspaper to report that the buzz of the bumble bee was pitched at the C sharp below middle C, but two years later he undertook some more research which showed that the pitch had gone up by a semitone to the D below middle C.

Tony Pristavec, concerts manager of Victor Hochhauser Ltd, was relieved at the news because, he said, it was obvious that the humble bumble bee had given up the annoying practice of performing at 'baroque' pitch. Another correspondent pointed out that because of its physical characteristics – huge body, narrow wings etc. – the bumble bee should not be capable of flight, aerodynamically speaking. 'Is it not therefore conceivable that, in keeping with modern technology, this amiable insect has increased its engine power with a consequent rise in pitch?', he inquired.

A former resident of Madras recalled how, in 1934, a military funeral was savagely dispersed by wild bees disturbed from their residence near the top of the cathedral. They had apparently been angered by the band playing Handel's Dead March in *Saul*.

A HIVE OF THEIR OWN

An American couple who moved into their new house in Florida found honey oozing down the walls and forming pools on the floors. Bees had invaded the cavity walls and ceiling spaces.

ILLEGAL IMMIGRANTS

Millions of bees – and their 12,000 hives – were 'arrested' by police on the North Yorkshire Moors. The hives had been illegally concealed by beekeepers from other parts of Britain. Some had travelled 200 miles to the moors around Scarborough because of the high-quality honey which the bees produce from the local heather.

PITCH INVASION

An invasion of bees ended a football match in Bangui, capital of the Central African Republic, for the second time in a week. Players and officials had to run for shelter, while the angry fans blamed witch-doctors.

ALL MIXED UP ABOUT SEX

British scientists developed 'sexual confusion' techniques in the 1970s to control insect pests. They synthesized the female sex attractant of three species and placed the substance at random in infected areas so that the male insects were led off on a fruitless and frustrating quest. Meanwhile, the females remained equally frustrated and unfertilized.

Tests were carried out in Cyprus on the armyworm moth, which attacks cotton, potatoes, tomatoes and ground-nuts, in Kenya on the tropical warehouse moth which goes for stored foods and in Malawi on the red bollworm, a cotton pest. In all three cases, the insect-breeding rates dropped considerably. One of the scientists involved in the research said the original idea had been to lure male insects into traps and then destroy them. The sexual confusion method proved more humane and more effective, even though it must have taken a lot of fun out of the insects' short lives.

A similar technique was developed by scientists at the UK Agricultural and Food Research Council's laboratory to control the aphid, that most annoying of garden pests. They isolated the sex pheromone which the female releases to attract the male and discovered that it was a chemical compound called nepetalactol.

Using samples of nepetalactol produced in the laboratory, the scientists made traps in which the chemical was surrounded by water. When these were placed outside hop fields in Kent, male aphids flocked in from miles around, hovered till they were exhausted and then fell in the water and drowned.

THE ELIXIR OF YOUTH?

Chinese pharmacists have developed what is claimed to be a remarkable tonic by distilling male silk moths. According to legend, the emperors of China used to eat the moths many centuries ago to cure impotence and to prevent ageing.

STING IN THE MAIL

A deadly scorpion was taken into custody after being sent through the post to a woman in case it had to be produced as a live exhibit at an Old Bailey trial. The scorpion was a *hadogenes bicolor*, one of the most dangerous species and normally found in Africa. It was kept under guard at the home of an insect specialist who fed it on a special diet of meal worms and blowflies.

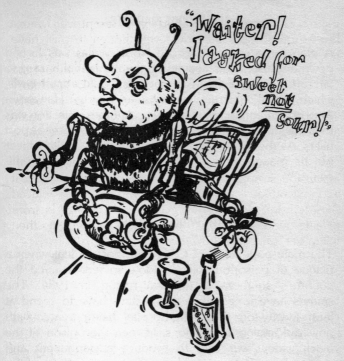

WORTH A DETOUR FOR THE SWEET COURSE

Australia's cucumber, melon and pumpkin producers have been facing financial disaster because the bees which normally pollinate their crops have been bypassing them in favour of flowers with a higher nectar content.

A researcher in Queensland University's horticulture department explained: 'People think that if a flower is there, a bee should pollinate it. But bees are a bit like people going to a restaurant – how far they travel will depend on their previous experience of how good the food is.'

119

HAZARDOUS MAGGOTS

A plan for a maggot farm in North Wales was turned down because it was deemed to be a potential hazard to aircraft. It was claimed the maggots would attract birds, which could obstruct runways at nearby Hawarden Airport and endanger flight safety. Another objection was that the smell from the maggot farm would upset airport users. As the local council's environmental health officer put it: 'Maggot breeding is fraught with potential difficulties.'

THE WIDOW'S CURSE

The male population of Chile had most to fear when a plague of poisonous black widow spiders invaded the country's southern agricultural region in 1984. The spiders have a nasty bite and victims have to spend at least twenty-four hours in hospital being treated with powerful analgesic injections. In men the poison of the black widow was said to produce a permanent and extremely painful erection for as long as the effects of the poison lasted. It is this condition which explains the colloquial Chilean expression for the local Don Juans: 'Stung by a spider'.

CAUGHT BY THE FUZZ

An insect which hunts by disguising itself as its own prey was discovered by biologists at Cornell University, New York. The predator is the lacewing larva, which preys on wingless aphids found on the leaves of alder trees.

The scientists discovered that when a lacewing larva

has killed an aphid it tears some of the fuzzy material from the body of its victim and wraps itself in this disguise to wait for the next unsuspecting aphid to pass its way.

IT'LL ALL END IN TEARS

One of the hazards of salmon farming is the prevalence of sea lice which attach themselves to the fish and can cause disease and death. But tests in Norway and the Faeroes found that the lice could be banished by the simple expedient of dangling a bag of sliced onions in the salmon cage. At first the Norwegians found that the onions had little effect but after a few weeks the lice stopped settling on the fish.

A similar result was noted when salmon farmers in the Shetland Islands adopted the same technique. But, to put the experiment on a more scientific basis, they commissioned a three-year study of the long-term effects of onions in salmon cages. What the salmon think about the smell of onions has not yet been established.

NEST EGG POACHED

A Kenyan farmer who buried banknotes worth £100 which he had saved for his wedding found that they had all been eaten by ants when he came to dig them up.

EXPENSIVE TASTES AT THE ZOO

It costs £15 to feed an ant for a year at London's zoo in Regent's Park, which compares with £6,000 for an elephant. As one correspondent in *The Times* pointed out, this implies a calorific equivalence between 400 ants and one elephant. It also suggests that it is not surprising the zoo has been making an annual loss of £5 million if it has to fork out £15 a year for every ant on the premises.

GLASNOST IN THE FOREST

Reflecting a more open, compassionate society, the Soviet Union established a sanctuary for ants on 1,600 acres of pine forest near Moscow. According to Radio Moscow, all tree-felling, hunting and camping in the area were banned to enable the first colonies to build up their strength.

ORDEAL IN ORBIT

The first ants in space did not survive their experience. About 100 of them went into orbit in the Challenger space shuttle on a flight in 1983, travelling in a special canister for an experiment by New Jersey schoolchildren. The cause of death was not discovered, but perhaps they just got bored.

DENIZENS OF THE DEEP

... including the dolphins who speak in a Hungarian accent ... the musical whale that liked Vivaldi ... thoughts on the lifestyle of a goldfish ... the pike who couldn't open a sardine tin ... the jellyfish who wobbled into space ... and the toads who ran foul of the US Drug Enforcement Agency.

ENGLISH AS SHE IS WHISTLED

Dolphins can speak in a Hungarian accent, according to a Californian professor of neuro-physiology who has studied the animals for more than twenty years. He spent two years trying to communicate with two dolphins called Joe and Rosie, whom he kept in a pool at a marine world near San Francisco.

He was unable to say which dolphin had spoken first, but one of them had demanded, 'Throw me the ball' with a distinctly Hungarian intonation. The professor was sure that the words came from one of the dolphins and not from a Hungarian colleague in his research team. It was simply that the dolphins had picked up his accent.

Other researchers, however, theorized that the Hungarian scientist's words had somehow got mixed up in the computerized underwater loudspeakers used in the research. Be that as it may, a psychologist at the University of Hawaii claimed that his pair of dolphins could understand English grammar. He taught them thirty words and they would obey instructions, using this vocabulary in hundreds of combinations. In one experiment, he reported, one of the dolphins immediately understood a new way of using the word 'in', proving a rudimentary knowledge of grammatical rules. Dolphins could indeed be good linguists because the various clicks, whistles and grating noises which they make among themselves are regarded by some scientists as a distinctive language.

FREDDIE, THE AMBLE ANGLER

An apparently gregarious Atlantic bottle-nose dolphin called Freddie arrived in the small port of Amble in Northumberland in 1987 and immediately boosted the town's tourist business. People flocked from miles around to see Freddie, who seemed to revel in all the attention he was getting.

But one dolphin expert was not so sure and thought Freddie was being harassed by the tourists. 'Freddie may give the impression of liking human contact, but the only reason he is in Amble is because the Coquet is a superb salmon river and he's a superb fisherman. Human contact is secondary.'

Freddie's appearance did spark off some medical controversy as to whether contact with dolphins could be good for humans. One doctor thought that it could become a recognized form of treatment for depression in the future, but a spokesman for the Royal College of Psychiatry dismissed this theory as 'a case of suggestibility'. He added: 'Any positive effect depressives feel they derive from swimming with dolphins will have more to do with the fact that depressed people usually tend to be remarkably inactive.'

TORPEDOING A RUMOUR

It sounds like a good idea, but the US Navy has denied that it trained dolphins for underwater attacks on enemy divers and ships.

NAVIGATION SCHOOL

A school of dolphins guided two shipwrecked sailors and helped them to swim to safety in rough seas off the coast of Indonesia in 1988. They were crewmen on an oil tanker which sank off Java and were not spotted by rescue teams which saved most of their colleagues. But the dolphins nudged and guided the two sailors, wearing lifejackets, to a small island off an Indonesian nature reserve.

WATER MUSIC

A musical whale called Fritz, trapped in a German harbour for more than five days, was enticed by the strains of Chopin and Vivaldi played by members of the Greenpeace environmental group and managed to swim to freedom in the North Sea.

FIRST FLIPPER

Sammy the seal was an unusual first-footer during the Hogmanay season at North Berwick in Scotland in 1978. He was observed several times emerging from the Firth of Forth and taking to the streets, apparently attracted by the Christmas lights. One local fisherman said: 'He may have been looking for human company. Young seals can become quite attached to humans and will follow them closely.'

PIONEER PILOT

A young female pilot whale with the rather unimaginative name of PW made medical history in the USA in 1982 by receiving physiotherapy. PW was found on a Cape Cod beach, the only one of sixty stranded whales to show any sign of life.

She was rushed to an aquarium in a water bed and it was discovered that her tail muscles had been partially paralysed, making it impossible for her to swim. The chief physiotherapist at the local hospital was called for and he decided to try electric shock treatment. PW responded with a few twitches, and the doctors went on to construct a special remote-controlled battery pack to help rejuvenate PW's injured tail.

SLIPPERY CUSTOMER IN COURT

A humble eel was the subject of a protracted series of court hearings in the days of the divided Germany. In 1976, a West German angler caught the eel while standing on the frozen Lankow lake. The lake happened to be in East German territory, although the bank from which he walked was in the West. There was no complaint from the East German authorities, but a West German court sentenced the angler to a fine of £125 for poaching – even though no such offence existed in the East German penal code. A higher court ruled that there had been no poaching and annulled the verdict. It was also pointed out by the court that a West German citizen could not be tried under East German law.

FIRST-CLASS FARE

With the benefit of hindsight, a consignment of king crabs from Alaska would probably not have chosen to fly by Air France on their way to new lives at Manchester and London Zoos in 1964.

The normal habitat for the huge crabs was the icy water around the Alaskan coast, so they had to be kept at near freezing temperatures during their journey. This was no problem till their flight reached Paris after the last connecting flight to London had departed.

There were no cold-storage facilities in the cargo centre, so the supervisor put the crabs in the refrigerator of the catering department, leaving strict instructions to his dayshift counterpart to put them on the first flight to London the following morning.

Unfortunately, the catering manager arrived at work first and, being French and finding his refrigerator miraculously filled with such a delicacy, decided to put king crab on the first-class menu for that day's Paris–New York flight. The passengers were delighted; the crabs made no comment. They were well advised to keep quiet because they were only travelling on one-way tickets.

SHELLING OUT FOR A NEW PET

Two enterprising New Yorkers went into the domestic pet business in the late 1970s with an unusual product in the shape of the tiny shore crab. They managed to persuade thousands of customers that the crab made a perfect companion and sold no less than 15,000 in a week.

IF MUSIC BE THE FOOD OF LOVE . . .

Houseboat dwellers in the Californian resort of Sausalito were kept awake every night by a loud humming noise. The source was tracked down to the plain-finned midshipman fish, otherwise known as the singing fish. The hum was said to be a natural phenomenon which occurs every year during the mating season.

THE ONE THAT DIDN'T GET AWAY

A 16lb salmon was responsible for the death of the angler who caught it. After he had caught the fish in the Wye near Hereford the angler collapsed and died on the river bank. His son said: 'It is ironic that this was the first salmon he had ever caught. Normally he fished for trout and had only just taken out a salmon licence. I think the excitement and the effort must have been too much for him, but I am sure he died a happy man because he had landed the fish when he collapsed. We are probably going to eat it. I think he would have approved.'

JAWS STRIKES GOLD

A voracious perch which acquired the name Jaws was blamed for eating 3,000 goldfish from a garden lake in Kent. Even though the owner of the lake was a champion angler, he had not been able to catch Jaws and, in desperation, called in the Army. A squad of five soldiers plus a Ferret armoured car and a machine gun arrived under the direction of the intrepid explorer Lieutenant Colonel John Blashford-Snell and set off two massive explosions, but still Jaws refused to surface.

Finally the Southern Water Authority was called in and engineers with an electric stunning device finally managed to net the elusive fish, which was promptly transferred to a smaller pond where he could not do so much damage.

Jaws' ferocious reputation may not have been entirely justified. He weighed less than a pound and as one of the Water Authority engineers commented: 'I doubt if he could have eaten all those goldfish. I rather think that herons could be responsible for much of the trouble.'

FLYING FISH

Britain hosted the first world championship goldfish race in 1991. They swam in special lanes in a pool in Weston Park, Shropshire. 'It's not cruel – there are no jockeys or whips,' said the organizer.

WORTH HIS WEIGHT IN GOLD

The finding of a Consumers' Association *Which?* survey that goldfish led a boring life and were generally ignored by their owners was described by one irate reader of *The Guardian* as 'an unfounded attack on the poor creature's sensibilities'.

'My own fish, Napoleon, leads a full and meaningful life in an airy and spacious Pyrex mixing bowl,' wrote P.E. Holdsworth of Southampton. 'During the two years we have been living together we have developed an intimate relationship based on mutual trust and respect and whenever I am absent for more than a few days he always stays with friends. Finally, I should like to point out that I spend more time with my goldfish than I do reading *Which?*'

MY GOLDFISH, MY GUINNESS

Goldfish are not renowned as gastronomic delicacies, but a few years ago there seemed to be a craze for people to swallow them whole. One man who swallowed six live goldfish at a pub in Stockport to win a £10 bet said he did not think it was cruel. 'Goldfish can't feel anything and they would be dead as soon as I swallowed them,' he maintained. The pub landlord said the feat was achieved in front of quite a crowd. 'He was drowning them with Guinness so they wouldn't feel a thing.'

But the achievement of a Californian man in a gold-fish-eating competition is unlikely to be beaten for a long time. He swallowed 501 fish in four hours to set a world record. He also won a rather bizarre prize in the shape of an aquarium, which must have been an extremely unsafe home for any fish unfortunate enough to take up residence in it.

TOO MUCH TO STOMACH

Scientists at the Gothenburg Maritime Museum's aquarium in Sweden have reported some of the strange objects found in the stomach of that most voracious of fish, the pike. They include money, spoons, rings, watches, a bottle of beer and even a tin of sardines. We all have problems in opening sardine tins, so it is not surprising to learn that even the pike with his sharp teeth had not managed to prise off the lid.

While on the subject of sardines, one recalls the occasion when pupils at a Camberwell school were asked to write not more than fifty words on the harmful effect of oil on fish. One eleven-year-old wrote: 'When my mum opened a tin of sardines last night it was full of oil and all the sardines were dead.'

SOUSED HERRING?

Thousands of fish which were believed to have been poisoned by industrial waste in Yugoslavia suddenly recovered because, it was found, they were only intoxicated by alcohol. The Podgorka plant had released a quantity of brandy into the Jadar river and made the fish behave strangely. Those of us who have sampled Yugoslavian brandy know the feeling.

FLOUNDERING TOWARDS THE FREEZER

Tomatoes are notoriously difficult to freeze but an Arctic fish, the winter flounder, has been enlisted in the search to produce a variety which can be frozen without losing taste or texture. An agricultural biotechnology company in California hit on the winter flounder because it can survive in water which is cold enough to freeze it without coming to any harm. The secret is that it has a special protein which affects the way the water in its body responds to temperatures below freezing.

Scientists developed a synthetic anti-freeze gene based on that of the flounder and inserted it into tomato plants. Initial tests were encouraging because the plants started producing the protein, but it remained to be seen what happened when the tomatoes were frozen. The technique, if successful, could also be applied to fruits like strawberries which just go mushy when they are defrosted.

PUTTING STRESS IN ITS PLAICE

A bio-chemist at Aberdeen University won an Open University M. Phil. degree after six years' part-time study which showed that plaice suffered less stress than other fish.

NOT HIS DAY

An angler who went fishing on the banks of the Rio Negro in the Amazon region was attacked by angry bees after he struck their nest while trying to free his line from a tree. To escape from the bees, he leaped into the river and was promptly eaten by piranha fish.

However, the boot was on the other fin in an incident at a night-club in the West Midlands when a man bit a piranha fish. He had been taking part in an 'endurance test' by putting his hand in a fish tank and had been bitten. The fish survived to bite another day.

SLIGHT WOBBLE FOR JELLYFISH, GIANT LEAP FOR FROGS

The jellyfish outnumbered the astronauts by 2,478 to 7 when the Columbia space shuttle lifted off in 1991 on a biological research mission. The aim was to study the effects of weightlessness on their gravity receptors, which are similar to those found in the inner ear of mammals. They were accompanied by twenty-nine white rats which were used to examine muscle function in the absence of gravity.

Six frogs accompanied the Japanese journalist Toyohiro Akiyama into space on his pioneering mission in a Soviet spacecraft. After the flight two of them were rushed to Japan to appear as the stars in a TV programme. The other four had a less fortunate fate and were sent to a molecular endocrinology laboratory in France, where they were dissected to see if weightlessness had any effect on their hearts and brains. The laboratory admitted that there was no special scientific reason why frogs were chosen in preference to any other species. 'I think it was because frogs are *sympathique*,' said the head of the laboratory. 'They have media appeal.'

On an earlier mission the sex life of the guppy fish in conditions of weightlessness came under scrutiny from the two Soviet cosmonauts on the orbiting Salyut-5 space station. As Tass delicately put it, a male and female guppy were taken into space to analyse 'the male's activity with regard to the female'.

SHAKY NUCLEAR REACTION

An invasion of giant jellyfish caused the shutdown of the Hunterston nuclear power station in Scotland for more than twenty-four hours. Technicians controlling the intake of sea-water for the plant's cooling system noticed that the instruments had started to wobble and were showing a rise in temperature.

'Wobble' was the right word because it turned out that sixty tonnes of jellyfish, some more than two foot wide, had been sucked into the system and had blocked the filters. Ironically the plant's reactor had just completed 305 days of continuous operation, setting a world record for its type. Had it not been for the jellyfish, the record would have been even more impressive.

CAUGHT ON THE JOB

A colony of Welsh toads became involved in the Government's job creation programme. Every year local naturalists in the Llandrindod Wells area set up patrols to help the toads across the road on their way to their spawning ground in a lake. But in 1978 they were helped by two graduates employed by Powys County Council under the jobs scheme.

The graduates went on patrol every night during the breeding season and caught the toads, marking them with a spot of dye to identify them and then releasing them in the spawning lake. The toads were then caught again when they staggered back from their spawning activities so that the researchers could record how long they had spent in the lake. They were co-operative subjects because, as the scientist in charge of the project observed, 'toads are not prima donnas'.

GUARD FROGS STOOD DOWN

American super-tadpoles became a yuppie craze on Tyneside in 1988. They were expected to grow into giant-size guard frogs which would deter the local cats from eating the goldfish in all the natty executive garden ponds. They became so popular that the price quickly went up from 75p to 99p per tadpole. But the garden centre which imported the tadpoles from Missouri recalled its stocks after being warned that they could eat most of Northumberland's newts, toads and indigenous frogs if they escaped.

The centre's aquatics supervisor said: 'There is a lot of executive housing round here. Some of the garden ponds are like lakes, and herons and cats stealing fish

Can I see your I.D, son?

are a terrible problem. This seemed an ideal solution because no cat in its right mind would go near this thing.'

The tadpoles – four inches long – were of the species *rana catesbeiana*, the largest known species of frog in North America, which has been known to eat small birds, young snakes, insects, crayfish, minnows, mice, voles and other frogs.

BAD TRIP FOR THE CANE TOADS

Police in Vancouver called for a ban on the import of cane toads into Canada because of their association with drug addicts in Australia. The toad produces a white toxin from its glands to ward off predators, and the fluid is so distasteful that it makes most animals run a mile. But in small doses, it is a powerful hallucinogenic, so much so that toad-licking became a trendy drug craze in California and quickly spread to other parts of the USA and Canada.

'When someone licks the toad his mouth and lips will become numb and he will feel intensely nauseous,' according to a spokesman for the US Drug Enforcement Agency. 'Within thirty minutes this induces a heightened trance-like state which lasts for six or seven hours and is meant to produce the same kind of hallucinations as LSD.'

An expert from the Natural History Museum in London said toad-lickers seemed to think that it was a clean, natural drug. 'But in fact the venom a cane toad produces contains a potentially lethal cocktail of substances that have been known to kill dogs,' he pointed out.

All the same, in the cane toads' native region, South America, their venom has been used for medicinal purposes and the Chinese have traditionally used dried toad to control their heartbeat.

VICTORY FOR MUSSEL-POWER

A US circuit judge ordered a stop to work on a $20 million copper-mining project in Wisconsin because of the presence of some rare species in the nearby Flambeau river. Among them were purple warty-back mussels, bullhead mussels, pygmy snaketail dragonflies, gilt dart minnows and river red horse minnows.

AND THE FAIRY LIVED HAPPILY EVER AFTER...

A rare fairy shrimp, less than an inch long, was saved from extinction on a Hampshire farm when naturalists built a diversionary tractor route around its home. The species likes to live in puddles and this particular shrimp found an ideal spot in the ruts made by the farmer's tractor. But local naturalists were alarmed when the farmer decided to fill in the ruts with rubble, so they built the new track around the shrimp's habitat and dug out the rubble. Thus encouraged, the fairy shrimp returned and bred successfully.

STRICTLY FOR THE BIRDS – PART 1

... and in particular a plethora of parrots, including the Norwegian bird sentenced to exile ... the Amazon parrot who croaked like a frog ... the Spanish parrot who was definitely *difunto* ... and the parrot purged by the late President Ceauşescu ... plus the noisy Swedish woodpecker who was reported to the police ... the blue tit who took a dislike to the British Rail timetable ... and the owl who joined in choir practice at Chichester Cathedral.

SICK OF A PARROT

Norway's most famous parrot is Jokko, a 50-year-old bird who was at the centre of a court action. Jokko enjoyed sitting in her cage in the garden of her home in the suburbs of Oslo during the long days of summer, but the neighbours were not so sure.

One of them brought a court action against Jokko, claiming that her squawking was like 'daggers in the stomach' and wanted to have her evicted or, at least, confined indoors to a back room. In the end the parties agreed to an out-of-court settlement in which Jokko was

139

to be kept out of sight from the neighbours and 'sentenced' to spend every other weekend during the summer and the whole of June away from home.

Jokko was not too upset by the settlement because she was used to spending the summer with her human 'grandmother' at a nearby holiday village in any case. But for her first visit to the village as a 'convict' she was given a special welcome with her own Norwegian-style chalet and a mini-suitcase full of the best bird seed.

Jokko is undoubtedly a talented bird. She can whistle the 'Internationale', although the pitch tends to go haywire after about four bars, and she tends to become rather confused about her sex when she wolf-whistles at an attractive girl passing by. She has also picked up the type of whistling noise used by dog-owners when summoning their charges, confusing most of the pooches in her part of Oslo. And when she sees a strange cat, she bleats like a goat.

Jokko is also quite a talkative bird when she puts her mind to it. She has been known to say the Norwegian equivalent of 'Have a nice day' or 'You don't say!' when the ladies get together in the holiday village for a good gossip over the morning coffee.

Earlier in her career, Jokko lived in a flower shop, where she learned to imitate the sound of a car braking or hooting. Hearing the sound of hooting, drivers visiting the shop used to think their delivery vans were causing an obstruction and hurried out into the street. It was then they heard the hooting coming from inside the shop ...

NICE LITTLE NEST EGGS

A parrot with the unremarkable name of Polly was left £5,000 in the will of an elderly lady in Harrogate. She made it clear in the will that the legacy was designed to ensure that Polly would continue to live in the manner to which she had become accustomed. It sounds a rather generous bequest because £5,000 represents rather a lot of birdseed – but then parrots do live to a ripe old age.

A slightly less generous bequest came from a Gloucestershire jazz enthusiast who left £2,000 to his two African grey parrots Ella and Louis (named after Ella Fitzgerald and Louis Armstrong). As a member of the family commented: 'It's enough to keep them in birdseed for at least 100 years.'

PHEW, WHAT A FREEZER!

All sorts of strange happenings hit the headlines during a cold snap. In the Arctic weather of early 1987, a parrot flew with remarkable precision into the intensive care unit of a Taunton hospital and was thawed out by the nurses before being handed over to the RSPCA. Around the same time, reports from Salzburg in Austria said the weather was so cold that hens' eggs were exploding as soon as they were laid.

A DEFINITELY DEFUNCT PARROT

John Cleese has immortalized the parrot which was definitely deceased, bereft of life, demised, passed on and gone to meet its Maker. His words were echoed in a Spanish court case by a judge who proclaimed in his summing-up: 'The parrot is deceased and cannot be revived.' But the learned judge set a useful precedent when he assessed the value of a dead parrot at 150,000 pesetas (£815).

This particular bird became definitely *difunto* in 1989 in a Barcelona hospital. It happened after his owner's mother developed an allergy and the doctor suspected that the parrot might be to blame. He suggested that the bird should have a blood test and that the test should be done by a doctor rather than a vet – unwise advice, as it turned out.

According to the owner, doctors virtually suffocated the parrot by putting a towel over its head and taking out six times as much blood as they were told to. Finally a consultant ordered that the bird should be put out of its misery. The dead bird was put in a freezer pending an autopsy, but it turned out that the deep freezing had made it impossible to determine the cause of death.

The owner lodged a claim for one million pesetas (£5,400) against the hospital and the doctor, which was based partly on the fact that the parrot could talk. But the judge ruled that the bird did not talk, it merely 'articulated sounds similar to those of people'. If the parrot had been able to talk, he added, it would have complained about its treatment.

OFF TO THE PALACE?

A patriotic green parrot called Benny was last seen on the sixteenth fairway of the Craigmillar Park course in Edinburgh after flying out of his kitchen window. Benny's owner reported that he had never talked but showed a marked interest in royalty.

'He is very interested when I talk about the Queen and I have taught him to curtsey,' she said. 'He makes cooing noises when he hears the Queen's name on TV.' It is not reported whether the hunt for Benny extended to Holyrood House, the Queen's official residence in Scotland.

THE CHATTERING CLASSES

A remarkable galaxy of talent among the parrot fraternity was assembled at the National Exhibition of Cage and Aviary Birds in Birmingham. Elected Britain's champion talking bird was Basil, a yellow-fronted Amazon parrot from Nuneaton who was able to bark like a dog, croak like a frog, crow like a cock, bleep like a telephone, cry like a baby, say (predictably) 'Who's a pretty boy?' and

143

re-enact the Charge of the Light Brigade with trumpet calls.

Among Basil's opponents were Pepper, a bilingual African grey parrot from Bury St Edmunds, who was able to say 'Good morning' in Japanese and imitate the call of the Chinese female quail and Billy Briggs, a pied cockatiel from Tenby, who had the unnerving habit of shouting 'Show us your knickers!' at passers-by. Another big draw was a talented Australian sulphur-crested cockatoo named Tommy. He was the star of a troupe of performing parrots and his feats included pedalling a tricycle and riding a chariot.

CONTEMPT OF COURT?

Three magistrates at a court in Highbury, North London, were alarmed when an African grey parrot which was an exhibit in a case against a pet-shop owner suddenly exclaimed: 'F*** off'. Unflustered, the magistrates' clerk told him: 'We'll be calling you later.'

The shop owner denied three summonses under the Trade Descriptions Act alleging that he had sold a parrot for £225, claiming that it was only five months old and suitable for talking. But the parrot proved to be an adult and would not utter a word.

The parrot produced in court was said to be from the same batch, but made no further intervention in the proceedings. He retired with the magistrates, who dismissed the summonses.

PARROT PURGE

A parrot owned by Romania's late President Nicolae Ceauşescu enjoyed a lavish lifestyle in the dictator's palace at Snagov. But when the president was away, the servants used to pass the time trying to teach the parrot to insult his owner. Despite intensive coaching, though, it remained silent until one day when Ceauşescu chaired a meeting in the room where the parrot lived.

The proceedings were brought to a sudden halt when the parrot flapped his wings and screeched: 'Stupid Nico, stupid Nico'. By the following day the parrot and cage had disappeared and were never seen again.

SHOPPING THE SHOPLIFTER

A young Texan man ended up in jail for theft because he was 'shopped' by a thirteen-year-old talking parrot named Eric, a popular member of the staff at a Houston shoe shop who delighted customers with his conversational abilities, until one day when he was stolen. When detectives visited the apartment of a nineteen-year-old man who was on probation for other offences, the parrot promptly identified himself, proclaiming 'Hello Eric', then adding 'Hello Laura'.

Police checked up the reports of stolen parrots and found the name of Laura Lancaster Bates, who owned the shoe shop. 'I didn't have to identify him,' said Ms Bates. 'He identified me.' The clincher came when Ms Bates entered the police station. Eric became very excited, flapped his wings vigorously and started swinging violently on his perch. Finally he screamed: 'Laura!'. The case was solved.

CLEANING UP THEIR ACT

Women visitors to Colchester Zoo used to be embarrassed by a contingent of parrots who had an unsubtle chat-up line of the 'Take off your knickers and give us a kiss' variety. The birds, predictably enough, had been coached by pupils of nearby boys' schools.

By way of counter-measures, the zoo authorities called in a local ventriloquist and her toy duck, Nelly, who together indulged in rather more refined conversation with the parrots. However, it was considered to be only a matter of time before the school boys returned to the bad-taste offensive.

A MYNAH PUNCTUALITY PROBLEM

Swiss railways have an enviable punctuality record but a mynah bird who lived opposite a suburban station in Berne was actually responsible for making trains leave before time (which can be just as annoying as a train running late). The bird had got so accustomed to hearing the sound of the conductor's whistle giving drivers the 'right away' that it started to imitate the sound, causing trains to set off before their scheduled departure time. As a result, drivers were instructed to make sure that they were given a hand signal as well as a whistle before taking their trains out.

NOT SUCH A PRETTY BOY

It took three policemen to catch Jacko, a four-year-old green-winged macaw who escaped from a Luton pet shop and had nineteen hours on the run. He was tracked down to a thirty-foot pine tree, where the police tempted him with a packet of peanuts. 'Come on Jacko, who's a pretty boy?' said one policeman, holding out a handful of nuts.

'F*** off,' came the prompt reply from Jacko before he was finally grabbed from his perch and bundled into a police van. 'I suppose we could have arrested Jacko for using foul and abusive language,' said a police spokesman later. 'But we decided to let him off with a warning.'

GALLANTRY IN THE GULF

Six singing but unsung heroes of the Gulf war were a squad of parakeets from Gibraltar. They were conscripted to serve on HMS Manchester as part of the vessel's chemical protection system – in much the same way that canaries are used in coal mines to detect gas. As a Navy spokesman explained: 'Despite our dependence on electronics, animals are still more reliable. The St George's flight, as they were known, served with great distinction under the leadership of Captain Joey.'

The birds were awarded the ship's gallantry medal before they were piped ashore and welcomed back by the children of a service school in Gibraltar, from whose aviary they had been press-ganged.

TOP OF THE PECKING ORDER

A noisy Swedish woodpecker was reported to the police, a dozen government departments and even insurance companies. A woman living in a Stockholm suburb complained that the woodpecker had made her life a misery for three years and she wanted it to be shot – even though it was a protected species. The woodpecker and its chicks had pecked holes in her wooden house and at one time she had been forced to sleep away from home. She tried spraying them with water to no avail. Then she threw a garden chair at them but it hit a power line. Early one morning she had opened the bedroom and screamed: 'Go away'.

'People must think I'm crazy,' said the aggrieved resident. 'Imagine reporting a woodpecker to the police.' Government officials suggested putting up a line of dummy eagles to scare the woodpecker away. 'But the neighbours would think I had gone completely off my rocker,' explained the woman, adding that 'the insurance company would pay only if the woodpecker attacked the house from inside.'

RIDDLERS ON THE ROOF

Woodpeckers in the Hampshire village of Tangley ran up a £3,000 bill for the local church after riddling its shingled steeple with hundreds of holes. The shingles had already been renewed after similar attacks five years earlier, and the Royal Society for the Protection of Birds thought there was nothing that could be done to prevent yet another recurrence.

Ironically, the new shingles which the birds seemed to favour had been treated with an anti-insect preservative, so it is unlikely that they would have found many grubs in them. More frequent ringing of the church's Henry VIII bell was rejected as a bird-scaring solution and it looked as if the only solution was an alternative – and more expensive – method of roof-cladding.

THANKS FOR THE MEMORY

A budgerigar with a good memory found its way home by repeating its telephone number. The year-old bird had spent eleven days in the wild after flying away from its home in Nottingham before being found by a lorry driver, who took it home. The bird kept repeating the number 223723, so the driver dialled it and discovered that it was indeed that of the anxious owner.

Another budgerigar called Poppy escaped from her home at Codrington near Bristol and was captured at a nearby village when she chirped her name and address. By the time she returned home her owners had installed a replacement budgie called Sammy. Poppy's wings have now been clipped to prevent her from popping out again.

Not to be outdone, a ten-year-old budgerigar was taught to sign off BBC Radio London's 'Up Your Street' programme in a Geordie accent. Why not Cockney?

UNKINDEST CUT

A motorist explained to Hampshire police that he had parked illegally outside a Southampton vet's surgery because his budgie's vasectomy took longer than expected'.

SHREDDING THE EVIDENCE

The tiny blue tit, a welcome visitor to our bird-tables in the winter, can also be an extremely destructive bird when it puts its mind to it. The British Trust for Ornithology carried out a survey into paper-tearing tits in 1950 and attracted more than 2,400 reports of incidents the previous year. The BTO discovered, for instance, that there had been 1,560 cases of tits attacking wallpaper 199 involving newspapers and magazines and 106 on lampshades.

No less than twenty blue tits flew into the chapel at Winchester school and shredded all the paper in sight including some open books. And at Scarborough railway station, a porter heard what he thought was a rat at work one night and shone his flashlight to discover a blue tit engaged in ripping up a timetable. As a British Rail timetable is often only of academic interest, it was probably a sensible move.

CRACKING THE COLOUR CODE

Blue tits are also well known for their skill in piercing milk-bottle tops. But one correspondent in *The Times* found that they can be discriminating as well. Dr Jack Crosby reported that his household took ordinary creamy milk (plain silver top) and skimmed milk (blue and silver). Over eight consecutive days nine out of sixteen silver tops were thoroughly broken into but none of the seventeen blue tops. The odds against this being chance were put at about 1,000 to one.

Then Dr Crosby switched the tops on four bottles. The two silver tops had no more than a small hole pierced in them because the tits discovered that the milk was inferior. But the birds were not that intelligent because the blue tops on the two creamy bottles were untouched

FISHY STORIES

A talking raven, Karlusha, kept winter anglers near Minsk
in the USSR entertained by announcing their catches.
Karlusha could recognize most of the fish caught and her
owner said she had a vocabulary of about sixty words.

PLUGGING AWAY AT A WATER PROBLEM

Rooks like to have a bath now and again, particularly in
hot weather, so it was only a matter of time before they
learned what bathplugs are for. Scientists at the
University of St Andrew's discovered that the birds could
pick up plugs, position them in a plughole and then bath
or drink in the resulting pool of water.

It happened in an aviary housing four captive rooks. It
had six drainage holes distributed around the concrete
floor, but only two of these normally removed water. At
first just one plug was left in the aviary and it was noticed
later that it had been perfectly positioned in one of the
drain holes and a shallow pool of water had accumul-
ated.

The researchers removed the plug but over the next
nine days it ended up in the plughole on five more
occasions. One of the birds was observed to pick up the
plug between the tips of its beak mandibles, using the
metal ring on the top, carry it to the plughole and drop it
straight in.

Later experiments showed no less than 477 cases of
plug-moving, but the holes which were used were almost
exclusively the two which actually allowed water to flow
out.

OSWALD'S CLOISTERED EXISTENCE

Among the side-effects of the hurricane in south-east England in October 1987 was the arrival of a young eagle owl who was blown into the cloisters of Chichester Cathedral. Quickly named Oswald, he was befriended by the organist and choristers and made himself at home by perching on an organ pipe and joining in the choir practice.

Oswald was so out of tune that his presence could no longer be tolerated in such a centre of musical excellence and a policeman was summoned to evict him. But honours were even, because before Oswald was finally captured and taken to a nearby animal sanctuary, he managed to bite the policeman.

OFF-KEY OWLS

The brother of the famous eighteenth century naturalist Gilbert White of Selborne discovered that all the owls in his Hampshire village hooted in the key of B flat. A neighbour of Gilbert White, who had a 'nice ear', found a distinct lack of harmony among the owls in his village because they hooted in three different keys: G flat, A flat and B flat.

WATER – THE IDEAL TURN-ON

A regime of cold showers is traditionally supposed to quell the passions of public-school boys. But they have been used to have just the opposite effect on a flock of frigid flamingoes.

In twelve years, thirty-seven Chilean flamingoes at the

Wildfowl and Wetlands Trust centre at Martin Mere in Lancashire produced only one chick. But after the trust installed a £4 water sprinkler on their island they quickly started to mate and build nests. 'When we started it they were terrified and all ran away,' said a spokeswoman for the trust. 'Now they fight for position.' Quite apart from any erotic effect the cold showers may have had, it seems that the water softened the mud and made it easier for the birds to build nests.

KICKING THE ADDITIVE HABIT

Any time now, the pink flamingoes at the Wildfowl and Wetlands Trust's Slimbridge centre are expected to turn white. Since 1991 scientists have been feeding the birds an experimental diet lacking in canthaxanthin, an ingredient which is thought to give them their salmon-pink colour.

In the wild, flamingoes obtain their canthaxanthin from shrimps and molluscs, but the Slimbridge birds were fed a synthetic version of canthaxanthin, now threatened by new health regulations. The scientists want to see how the birds fare on an additive-free diet and then, after a year, they will try another artificial pigment, astaxanthin.

Apart from the effect on the birds' health, the researchers want to see if a change in the colour of their plumage will affect their mating rituals.

NOT A LEG TO STAND ON

A silly-season correspondence in *New Scientist* tackled a question which has long baffled ornithologists: why do flamingoes stand on only one leg? One reader suggested that they do not always stand on the same leg but alternate from one to another to eliminate the risk of getting stuck in the mud. A more flippant theory came from a reader in Japan, who argued that it was to halve the frequency with which ducks bumped into them.

And a correspondent from University College, Dublin, pointed out that by holding one leg against its body the flamingo could reduce the distance the blood had to travel against the force of gravity. 'Standing on each leg alternately prevents blood collecting in the feet,' he suggested.

The same subject was discussed by readers of *The Guardian*, one of whom pointed out that the legs and feet of flamingoes have a high surface-area-to-mass ratio and are therefore susceptible to heat loss, particularly if the birds stand still for periods with their feet and legs in the water. So they stand with one leg tucked into the feathers of the lower body, reducing potential heat loss by fifty per cent. But this theory was discounted by a scientist at the Wildfowl and Wetlands Trust, who pointed out that flamingoes also stand on one leg in the summer, when there is no heat-loss problem.

GUMMING UP THE GUARDS

The US 32nd Air Defense Command enlisted 900 geese to guard military installations in Germany. It was, according to a spokesman, an 'optimized deployment concept' and followed a study carried out under the codename 'Gooses' (Goose Operational and Strategic Effectiveness Study). But things did not go according to plan. The geese were posted as guards under the control of an officer armed with a whistle and a rubber uncheon. Sadly, though, he noticed that the geese were excreting red, balloon-like droppings which made a small popping sound. Some potential intruder, in an attempt to stop them honking, had found that geese were partial to bubble gum.

THE WICKED SQUIRE WHO GOT A BIG HISS

The actor cast as the wicked squire for a performance of the pantomime Mother Goose in Yorkshire had to be treated in hospital for a sword wound after being attacked by a goose during a duel scene. The goose, which had been introduced into the cast to give a touch of realism, quite appropriately took an instant dislike to the squire, whose injury needed two stitches. The goose was dropped from the cast.

FEATHERED TRAFFIC WARDENS

A wine shop owner in the tourist village of Grinzing, just outside Vienna, was annoyed by the way that traffic rushed through the narrow winding streets. So he turned a flock of seven geese out into the streets to slow the traffic down. The drivers immediately reduced speed – but that could have been because they were distracted by the pretty goose girl who was escorting the birds.

THE CALL OF THE BRIGHT LIGHTS

The Canada goose is a remarkably successful introduced species in Britain. It has also acquired a nuisance value, particularly in London's parks where it has taken to roosting on restaurant tables and leaving its visiting cards behind (it produces a large dropping every three or four minutes). A similar problem occurred in its native Canada some years ago. So a humane society in Toronto, thinking it was doing the right thing, captured a dozen pairs of local geese and transported them 250 miles to Lake Erie to be released in a wildlife sanctuary. On the return journey, the driver of the now empty truck noticed twenty-four low-flying geese overtaking him on the way back to their soft city life in Toronto.

A British attempt to limit the growth of the Canada goose population involved the use of hard-boiled eggs. Researchers at the Agricultural Research Council's centre at Great Linford in Buckinghamshire discovered that if they removed goose eggs from the nest, hard-boiled them and then replaced them in the nest the geese would continue to sit without noticing anything suspicious. They were also fooled by dummy wooden eggs. By the time the geese realized that the eggs were never going to hatch it was too late in the season for them to produce a new clutch.

OUT FOR A GUCK

An ornithological curiosity known as a 'guck' saw the light of day on a farm in Sussex in 1983. It resulted from the crossing of a gander and a duck and was thought to be the first of its kind, although the Wildfowl Trust reported previous crossings of a goose and a swan.

FAME FOR A FEATHERED FAMILY

A family of ducks caused annual traffic jams in the heart of Tokyo during the 1980s. Each year a duck hatched out her family in a man-made pond in front of the Mitsui Trading Company's headquarters. Then, when it was time for the ducklings to learn to fly, police halted traffic on an eight-lane highway as the mother duck escorted them across to the moat of the Imperial Palace.

They really achieved fame in 1986 when a TV documentary about the mother duck was screened on New Year's Day, a holiday which emphasizes family life for the Japanese. Later that year 25,000 people turned up in front of the Mitsui building in the hope of seeing the birds set off on their adventurous journey and several people fell into the pond before guards roped it off. The event was also covered by 100 reporters and photographers from all the country's main newspapers and TV networks.

After the documentary was first shown, Nippon Television responded to public demand by screening three repeats. It also received 2,000 letters, many from appreciative mothers saying how much they had learned from the mother duck.

MURDER AT THE PET SHOW

A duck taking part in the National Unusual Pet Show at a wildlife park near Canterbury ate one of the other entrants, a ten-inch pet slug. The duck, named Quackers, was observed looking into a bucket and it was not till a small boy asked where his slug was that the evil deed was discovered.

OH, WHAT A SURPRISE

A duck took revenge on a hunter in New Zealand. It dived out of the sky, knocking him out and leaving him with two lovely black eyes, a broken nose and cracked glasses.

CRASH COURSE ON THE CAMPUS

A mallard duck got itself trapped in the junior common room at York University, appropriately enough during the annual conference of the Royal Society for the Protection of Birds. But the sight of 1,000 ornithologists forced it to crash-dive through a window and escape to the safety of the campus, where it was later seen recovering from a very sore head.

DONALD IN DISGRACE

The Youth Board in Helsinki ruled in the late 1970s that Donald Duck was not suitable reading for children and cancelled library subscriptions for Donald Duck comics. The board complained that Donald was unduly bourgeois. It also criticized pictures of naked ducks, stories about incomplete families, harmful attitudes towards children and Donald's common-law marriage.

STRICTLY FOR THE BIRDS – PART 2

... including the sobering story of the drunken Cumbrian ducks ... the low-flying turkeys of Arkansas ... the sexual plight of the pelicans in St James's Park ... the pheasant's revolt ... and the pigeon who became the star of the stud farm.

ONLY THERE FOR THE BEER

Pubs have some pretty unlikely names, but one of the most offbeat is the Drunken Duck at Burrowgate in the Lake District. The story of how it got its name is a cautionary tale. One day the landlord threw away some stale beer, which was promptly drunk by his wife's pet ducks, with rather violent effects. She found all the birds lying around apparently dead, so rather than waste them she started to pluck them, ready for the pot and the pub's 'special of the day'. Then, just as they were about to be popped in the oven, the ducks suddenly came to and emerged from their drunken stupor.

The horrified landlady immediately knitted them all little woolly vests to keep out the cold till their feathers

grew again. Which explains why the pub sign shows a happy duck staggering around wearing a woolly jumper.

DECIBEL RATING FOR A DAWN CHORUS

A Devon architect who claimed that his neighbour's noisy cockerel, Cocky, kept him awake at night won his case before Totnes magistrates. The court dismissed an appeal by the bird's owner against a noise abatement order, recommending that Cocky should have his wings clipped so that he could not fly into the trees and that he should be fenced in or otherwise controlled.

The architect complained that Cocky had made nights a misery for him and his wife. The bird's raucous crowing regularly woke him any time after 4 a.m. and he became so tired that he had to go to the doctor for sleeping tablets. A council environmental health officer took a sound reading at 5 a.m. and said Cocky clocked up a level of between fifty and sixty decibels.

Cocky's owner said: 'The council said I must catch him every night and put him in a sound-proof box, but he has never been handled. I would have to race about with a net every night to try and secure him.'

PLENTY TO CROW ABOUT

They seem to have a thing about noisy cockerels in Devon. The inspectors also got out their decibel-measuring equipment at Stoke near Hartland following complaints about the early-morning serenade by a bird called Corky, and Torridge District Council eventually served a noise-abatement order on his owners.

'I'll fight to keep my rooster,' Corky's owner declared. 'He hasn't had a fair hearing yet. He does crow early in the morning and wake everybody up, but that is what he is for. How can you stop a bird from crowing? He's only doing his job.

'Years ago in the countryside, before there were alarm clocks, everyone depended on the cockerels to get them up in the morning. What can I do? I can't just put him in the oven. I must stand up for the rights of the individual and fight against this bureaucracy.'

One of the neighbours who complained about Corky said his crowing was no different from a town noise like a car revving up outside the bedroom window. And a council spokesman said Corky would have to be 'distanced, insulated or contained away from the complainant'.

CHICKEN RUN

More than 30,000 chickens ran through the streets of three Brittany towns after egg producers freed them to protest against low prices. The police said dozens of birds were run over by passing cars, but there were no injuries to humans.

ON THE DOLE?

The Department of Bizarre Information, otherwise known as the Central Statistical Office, has produced figures showing that chickens outnumber people by more than two to one in the UK. But fewer than a quarter of them earn their living producing eggs, while half the human population goes out to work. The CSO also discovered the remarkable fact that in one year British chickens laid 13,561,975,000 eggs (or, if you prefer, about 250 per head of the human population).

THE COST OF CANNIBALISM

A study by the Poultry Research Centre into cannibalism and feather-pecking among chickens cost the British taxpayer £49,000, it emerged in a House of Commons written answer. A Conservative MP who raised the question said it was another case of wasteful spending. He cited a previous study by the centre, which spent £35,000 over five years investigating why chicken eggs break.

DANGER: LOW-FLYING TURKEYS

The annual Turkey Drop is a traditional, if controversial, sport in the Ozark Mountains region of Arkansas. Turkeys are not known for their flying ability, but the idea behind the sport is that a small low-flying aircraft makes several swoops over the town of Yellville and drops domestic turkeys on the assembled populace.

In theory each of the seventeen birds taking part in the festivities should spread its wings and make a graceful descent to the town square but in the past it hasn't always worked out like that. The event has sometimes been marred by deaths and injuries among the birds, and protests from turkey-lovers became so strong in the 1950s that it was decided to use frozen birds, throwing them out of the aircraft with small parachutes attached. But the frozen turkeys posed other hazards. One smashed through the roof of a resident's front porch, while another severely dented a car.

Another year the local Chamber of Commerce, which organizes the event, bought a flock of turkeys whose wings had been clipped. Not surprisingly, very few turkeys survived their 100 foot drop.

DYNAMIC DROPPINGS

Turkeys could be playing their part in the UK Government's campaign to find more environmentally-friendly ways of producing electricity. Plans have been submitted to the Department of Trade for a power station which would convert turkey droppings into enough electricity to supply 1,000 homes. The company behind the scheme reckons that Britain's million-plus turkeys could produce enough droppings to support more than five similar power stations.

The secret of the scheme is that the droppings would be broken down by 'anaerobic digestion' to produce methane fuel which would power the generators. Around sixty tonnes of droppings would be brought in daily from some thirty local farms. But what will happen over the Christmas period, when the demand for electricity is at its peak and, for one reason or another, there aren't many turkeys around?

PARLIAMENTARY PELICANS

The pelicans who live in St James's Park in London are something of an ecological anachronism. They normally enjoy life in a rather more tropical climate, which no doubt accounts for the fact that they have not laid an egg in London since the time of James I.

But at least, the House of Lords has taken an interest in their sexual plight; Lord Stodart of Leaston suggested the obvious solution that there might not be a male among them. Lord Stodart was the best qualified peer to talk about the pelicans because, he confessed, he used to talk to them. When he became a Member of Parliament in 1959 he practised his maiden speech by addressing the pelicans to the accompaniment of the dawn chorus as he walked through the park.

'Not a soul was looking and the pelicans seemed to be quite appreciative,' he recalled. 'Later I was told that I was not the only one who did that, although no one admitted it.' The maiden speech involved the Mental Health (Scotland) Bill, under which the police were to be allowed to detain for up to forty-eight hours any person deemed to be showing signs of eccentric behaviour (which could presumably include talking to pelicans) without informing relatives. But Lord Stodart succeeded in winning an amendment which limited the period of detention to twelve hours. 'From then on I have always rather felt for the pelicans,' he admitted.

THE TAIL WAGS THE DIG

Bird-lovers paid the owner of a JCB digger £180 a week to keep it off the road while a family of baby wagtails were reared on its engine. They hired a replacement vehicle so that the contractor could continue his work on the M3 extension in Hampshire.

The nest was discovered when the two parent birds were seen following the digger from its depot to the construction site. They apparently appreciated the warmth radiating from the engine and five fledglings were successfully hatched after the digger was 'grounded'. The only problem was that the new vehicle proved unreliable and yet another replacement had to be brought in.

THE EAGLES HAVE LANDED

Two eagles attacked an Aeroflot passenger aircraft over the northern Caucasus and chased it till it landed. The pilot took evasive action but the eagles struck again when the aircraft landed, leaving a nasty dent and scratches in its left wing.

THE PHEASANT'S REVOLT

A pheasant which had just been shot had its revenge on the wife of its assailant in its dying moments. The incident happened on a Hampshire estate during a shoot when the woman, an amateur artist, was sitting on her shooting stick sketching the landscape.

'I heard a shot, looked up and watched the pheasant falling towards me,' she recalled. 'There was nothing I could do to get out of the way because it was a muddy day and my boots were very heavy. I twisted to my right and it hit me in the back and winded me. I was very lucky because it could have broken my neck.'

The woman was treated in the casualty department at the local hospital and was discharged but had to return a few days later because she was experiencing severe pains. Doctors found that her spleen had been ruptured and she needed an operation. 'We were hoping we would get the pheasant,' said the surgeon. 'But I think she kept it and ate it as her final revenge.'

SOMETHING TO GROUSE ABOUT

A similar experience befell a marksman on Lord Bolton's estate in the Yorkshire Dales. He had just shot a grouse and was about to aim at a second when he was knocked unconscious and flung into the heather by the dead bird falling from the sky and hitting him in the face. He left the moor half-an-hour later nursing a cut lip and two black eyes.

'I took aim at the second bird but that is the last I remember because the dead one hit me straight in the face,' he said later. 'It was hard work convincing my wife that I had been battered by a dead grouse. You wouldn't believe how painful a 1½ lb grouse is when it hits you at 60 mph. But I ate it for dinner three nights later and it was delicious.'

ONCE BITTERN, TWICE SHY ...

The bittern, a member of the heron family, is a notoriously rare and retiring bird – an endangered species, in fact. But during a spell of very cold weather in the 1960s one bird, apparently desperate for food, joined a bus queue in Norfolk and pecked one of the passengers. It is not recorded whether the bird actually got on the bus.

STICKING INTO A SQUARE MEAL

The grey heron is usually a solitary feeder. But the easy meals provided by salmon and trout farms in Scotland have proved so attractive that the birds have started hunting in packs. To protect the fish, one farmer put nets over the holding pools but even then the herons got the better of him. At first the nets were a deterrent because the birds got tangled in them. But then they started collecting large sticks – just as if they were building their nests – and used them as platforms to push down the nets so that they could get at the fish once again.

BIRD CONTROL

The city fathers of Florence seem to have some strange hang-ups about the local animal life (see, for instance, 'Dress Code for Horses' on Page 57). Pigeons are a familiar part of everyday life in many cities, but in 1987 the Florentine health commissioner proposed that contraceptives should be prescribed for the local birds to keep down the numbers. The commissioner said he had received complaints that the birds were endangering citizens because they were infested with mites.

PESTERING THE PILGRIMS

They obviously have a preoccupation with pigeons in Italy. The authorities in the Vatican installed low-voltage electric wires to stop the birds flying over the entrance to St Peter's Basilica and damaging its priceless marble with their droppings. Officials said the shocks caused the pigeons no harm, but merely forced them to bombard the unsuspecting pilgrims in St Peter's Square instead.

SHOW ME THE WAY TO GO HOME ...

Judging by the numbers of racing pigeons one sees wandering aimlessly along footpaths on the coast of southern England, many of them are in no great hurry to get back to their native lofts. One bird which was supposed to be flying from France to Hereford rested so

long on a Russian ship that it got home two weeks after the race was over. A note from the ship's crew was attached to the bird's leg, explaining how they had looked after it.

TRIUMPH FOR OLD TECHNOLOGY

Those of us who use fax machines know how they can hang up sometimes, producing incomprehensible error messages. One high-tech communications company was more than somewhat embarrassed when a race was held between its latest fax machine and a homing pigeon. The task was to send a message from a hotel near Heathrow Airport to the pigeon's home in West Drayton, a mile away. The pigeon managed to get there before the message was successfully transmitted by the machine.

AIR-TAXI SERVICE

A plan to replace taxis by pigeons to ferry urgent medical specimens around the city was hatched by the Plymouth health authorities in 1977. A special loft was constructed at the city's Freedom Fields Hospital, which housed the central laboratory, and specimens were sent there by carrier pigeon from the Devonport Hospital, four miles away.

The economics of the scheme were attractive because it was estimated that the £25,000 a year spent on taxis would be reduced to only about £50 for pigeon food. It was, perhaps, not surprising that the scheme was devised because the health district's administrator was a pigeon fancier and one of the blood transfusion service drivers also had a pigeon loft. Even more to the point, the health district personnel officer was a Mr Steven Pidgen.

HOSPITALITY BUDGET CUTBACK

A Cheshire bird fancier was ordered by Stockport magistrates to cut back on his hospitality to a flock of pigeons. The local council asked for an order to stop him feeding up to eighty pigeons who visited his garden regularly to enjoy a gourmet meal.

The council's lawyer told the court: 'Because of them gathering like this, house guttering has been choked, walls defaced, washing contaminated and there has been a noise, nuisance and smell.' The court decided against a total ban but ordered the fancier to cut the birds' rations so that not more than five pigeons would be feeding at any time.

STAR OF THE STUD FARM

Pigeon racing may have been regarded as a working-class sport at one time, but now it has definitely moved upmarket. The most exclusive bird is De Smaragd II, who changed hands for £77,000 when he was bought by the owner of a pigeon stud farm near Loughborough. De Smaragd II who previously had Dutch owners – his name is Dutch for emerald – had enjoyed a distinguished racing career. He won the Barcelona International Race in 1988, flying 750 miles to his loft in Eindhoven at an average speed of 45 mph. Having gone to stud, De Smaragd no longer takes part in races but he is earning his keep by producing offspring which sell for up to £3,000.

ROMANCE FOR A DOVE OF PEACE

The authorities in China, anxious to bring Taiwan back to the 'motherland', hatched up a romantic plot to unite a Taiwanese male homing pigeon and a mainland female called Flower Raindrops.

The male bird had flown to Tianjin where it was wounded by hunters, but was nursed back to health and then sent to Beijing for the political 'wedding'. The

Beijing Evening News said the birds were mated on the day of the Lantern Festival which rounds off the New Year festivities and is celebrated on both sides of the Taiwan straits.

NOISY NEIGHBOURS

A housewife promised a High Court judge to find a new home for three noisy members of her suburban flock of birds – a peacock and two peahens. The mating season was about to begin and peafowl were particularly noisy, the judge was told. But it did seem rather hard that they were singled out for expulsion because the other residents of the two-acre estate included two cockerels, nine geese, thirty chickens, twenty ducks, plus a goat, which collectively could have made just as much noise.

THE TWITCHERS TWITCHED

A rare American visitor in the shape of a buff-breasted sandpiper was spotted on Pennington marshes in Hampshire in the autumn of 1991. And, as always happens with an unusual arrival, the 'twitchers' arrived in force armed with expensive telescopes, video recorders and binoculars ready to tick off this new species on their lists. The sandpiper arrived at dawn and started to feed ... but down swooped a sparrowhawk and carried off the unfortunate immigrant to provide itself with an unusual breakfast delicacy.

BIRD-BRAINED DISCOVERY

A year-long search by a British naturalist in Fiji for a bird thought to be extinct ended when it crashed on his head. The bird, the MacGillivray's petrel, had last been recorded 129 years earlier, but the naturalist lured one in from the sea at night using flashlights and recordings. It crashed on his head and, after examining the bird, he let it go – hopefully to remain undisturbed for the next 129 years.

MISCELLANEOUS MENAGERIE

... including some *Which?* research on the best buys among pets ... animals' TV-watching habits ... the laziest animals in the world ... the animals who help to compile the weather forecast ... and the goldfish who have acupuncture treatment to reduce stress.

PETS' TOP OF THE POPS

It made a change from washing machines and fridges when the Consumers' Association magazine *Which?* decided to turn its attention to pets. It even came up with a fairly predictable best buy – a dog – while cats came only third in popularity after horses and ponies.

The magazine analysed questionnaires covering 2,088 pets completed by 1,600 CA members. In typically thorough *Which?* style, the survey took into account the initial cost of the pet, its running costs and the amount of time taken in looking after it. It also compared a more intangible criterion – the amount of enjoyment each animal contributed to the household.

Dogs had the disadvantage of being fairly expensive initially and of having fairly high running costs. But dog-owners said they 'actively enjoyed' the company of their pets for an average of four hours a day. Cats, by contrast, were cheap initially although their running costs were also on the high side. But they provided their owners with only one hour, forty minutes' enjoyment every day.

Horses and ponies were expensive and costly to maintain, but they were more durable and were enjoyed much more than tortoises (which provided no more than ten minutes' delight for their owners every day).

Goldfish got a poor rating. Although they were very cheap to buy and feed, they provided only ten minutes' daily enjoyment to their owners and one goldfish owner in five admitted to ignoring the pet completely. Several respondents complained that tortoises 'failed to return love', while hamsters were said to be 'unresponsive, nocturnal and solitary'. Other pets covered by the survey included a hedgehog and a snail.

LEAGUE OF THE BIG SPENDERS

Confirming what we'd always guessed, another survey has shown how Britons pamper their pets. According to *Wild About Animals Magazine*, which surveyed 1,000 readers, a pet can cost its owner up to £10,000 during its lifetime. Dog-owners spend £9,000 on their animals over a twelve-year period, while a cat's average thirteen-year lifespan means a bill of £6,000. Cats in Scotland, the North-West and North-East have the most lavish lifestyle, with their owners spending an average of £10,000.

But a spokesman for the Kennel Club put the figures in perspective, pointing out that many people will spend more on alcohol in the twelve years of a dog's life. 'Walking a dog is better exercise,' he pointed out. The survey also uncovered some of the more unusual life-styles of British pets, including a dog and rabbit which sleep together, a kitten which likes vindaloo curry, and Noddy, an accident-prone budgerigar which crashed to a near-disaster on a test flight. According to Noddy's owner, he had been flying round the room when he fell into a narrow vase and had to be extracted by his legs, having pulled a muscle.

The survey named Brigitte Bardot as the top animal-loving personality, but she was closely followed by author Jilly Cooper, who commented that £10,000 per animal sounded very low for her family. 'We cook chicken for our pets and a dog-sitter is brought in when we go out,' she confessed.

RELATIVE VALUES

In yet another survey, conducted by Mori, no less than forty-nine per cent of the 1,230 people questioned said they owned a pet. When asked if they preferred their pets to their relatives, forty-six per cent of the owners agreed, while twenty-five per cent disagreed and the remainder offered no opinion. Mori added: 'Agreement that the British like their pets more than their relatives was wide-spread, never falling below four people in ten and in every group always considerably outnumbered those who disagreed.'

DEALING WITH THE DEAR DEPARTED

The only certainty about animal life is death. But the question of how the passing of one's favourite pet should be marked is not so easy to resolve. In the United States, there are some 500 cemeteries where furred and feathered loved ones are laid to rest, overseen by the National Association of Pet Cemeteries.

In Britain, by contrast, cemeteries for animals are still few and far between. One entrepreneur who set up in business as a pets' undertaker had an instant success and was asked to cremate fifty cats and dogs in his first three months, so he quickly invested in a £5,000 cremator to cope with his booming business. And staff at the Rossendale Pets Memorial Gardens in Lancashire said their cemetery was always kept busy, with several hundred animals buried there, including two budgerigars, a horse and a cow called Florence.

The need for animal cemeteries was also stressed during a planning application elsewhere in Lancashire. The developer said the cemetery would be tastefully laid out as a park, with trees and shrubs and headstones chosen to blend with the surrounding landscape. He added that clergymen could be found to conduct burial services if the owners requested, pointing out: 'They are held in Italy and approved by the Catholic Church there. It is a theological argument.'

TV GOING TO THE DOGS?

The *Radio Times* carried out a survey in conjunction with National Opinion Polls to study the TV viewing habits of the Great British Public. Apart from those findings which are beyond the remit of this volume – such as the fact that 2 million Britons indulge in love-making while the TV is on – it emerged from 8.5 million viewers that, in contrast to the population at large, their pets are watching more television than ever, with about half being described as 'active viewers'.

PENILE POTION

Penises from 1,000 New Zealand deer were sold to China to make an intriguing product called 'most precious three penis wine'. The wine, made by China's National Animal By-Products Corporation, was said to cure loss of memory, anaemia and shingles.

The powerful concoction was made from one powdered dog's penis and one from a seal, mixed with four from deer to make the wine, which was described as 'robust and nutritious'. It sold for about £1.75 a bottle and a powdered compound was also said to be available.

QUITE A LOT TO DECLARE

The Norwegian Customs authorities clamp down severely on any attempt to smuggle contraband alcohol into the country. But one Customs officer who suspected that a nervous traveller from Denmark was bringing in illicit booze was more than surprised when he opened the suitcase and discovered, instead, fifty canaries, six guinea pigs and a large rat.

THE TIME OF THEIR LIVES

The animal world has now been subjected to 'time budget analysis'. Or, stripping away the jargon, scientists have been trying to establish how animals spend their time. The laziest animal of all seems to be the spadefoot toad, found in the deserts of the south-western United States, which spends eleven months of the year underground doing nothing. Also, the ant, normally regarded as an extremely busy creature, actually spends only about twenty per cent of its time on the go and the rest just lazing round.

WHEN PETTING BECOMES RESPECTABLE

Pets can be good for you, according to an American survey. The study showed that pet owners recovering from a heart attack were more likely to survive than those who did not own a pet. When patients suffering from high blood pressure were monitored while stroking or talking to their pets, the pressure went down.

One British expert, Walter Beswick, senior vice-president of the British Veterinary Association, and many different types of people benefited from having pets – particularly elderly people living alone – and people who suffered from stress would often find the tactile qualities of an animal calming. 'Although most people would not find a snake attractive, our aversion to them is a cultivated response. An eight-foot python can be a beautiful creature and a good pet.'

CAPTAINS FIRST, DOGS AND CANARIES LAST

The captain of the doomed cruise ship *Oceanos*, which sank off the coast of South Africa in 1991, came in for some stick for apparently ignoring maritime tradition by leaving the vessel two-and-a-half hours before the last passengers were rescued. The last man on board was the cruise entertainment director, whose final duty on the bridge was to release the captain's dog and three canaries. 'The dog bit my finger but it went off in one of the lifeboats,' he reported later.

It was the same entertainment director who, between his rescue duties, boosted the morale of the passengers still on board with stirring piano performances of such inappropriate works as 'We Are Sailing' and 'Goodbye Love, Goodbye Happiness, I think I'm going to die'.

PREGNANT WARNING

Finnish and Swedish Air Force pilots were ordered not to fly too low to avoid disturbing pregnant reindeer, mink and other animals. 'The reindeer sometimes have miscarriages when fighters fly low,' according to a Finnish Air Force spokesman. The noise shocks also made mink miscarry or kill their young. So pilots were ordered to fly above 1,700 feet over mink farms between March and June.

ALL ANIMALS ARE EQUAL...

Haringey Council in North London caused a controversy with its decision to appoint an animal rights officer while it was said to have a list of 5,000 homeless and debts of £500 million. It was part of the council's drive to tackle 'speciesism' – discrimination by humans against another animal because it comes from a different species.

The new job was advertised at a salary of about £11,000 a year and it was made clear that applications from members of the Animal Liberation Front would be welcome. In the event more than 100 applications were received within just a few days. A spokesman said: 'The council has a policy of equal opportunity for people with criminal records. So that means someone with a conviction for a fire bombing or releasing animals from captivity will be considered.'

The council had already banned circuses with live animals as well as funfair sideshows offering goldfish as prizes and had apparently voted to spend £56,000 on a hostel for homeless cats.

It was thought that one of the new appointee's first jobs would be to inquire into the case of Minnie the mongoose, who escaped from the home of a Haringey family by nipping through the catflap. But it looked as if the animal rights officer would want to know why Minnie's owners taught her to perform various tricks, including roller-skating.

PHEW, WHAT A FORECAST!

Bill Foggitt has acquired a reputation as Britain's best-known amateur weatherman through his ability to read the signs of nature. He forecasts high winds when his black cat starts dashing madly round the kitchen, while sleepy flies mean that a wet spell is on the way. Garden spiders spin long webs before spells of dry and calm weather and a hovering kestrel means that bad weather is on the way (although, presumably, it might just be hungry).

BLESS THIS MOUSE...

More than thirty organizations, including the Royal Society for the Protection of Cruelty to Animals and the Pet Food Manufacturers' Association (not altogether a disinterested participant), have got together to run an annual Pet Week. The 1991 event was kicked off with a non-denominational pets' blessing service, followed by sponsored dog walks and cat shows. Owners were also able to show off some of their exotic pets, which included rats, tarantulas, pot-bellied pigs and African giant snails. Two snails were also blessed at a fundraising service for the RSPCA held in Cornwall.

EXIT, PURSUED BY A BEAR?

Actors and officials at the Regent's Park Open Air Theatre in London were alarmed at the prospect of the nearby London Zoo being closed down because the animals had got into the habit of producing some interesting sound effects. One lion apparently acquired the knack of doing its stuff when Bottom declares in *A Midsummer Night's Dream*: 'I will roar, that I will do any man's heart good to hear me.' The parakeets and parrots were said to join in when Bottom added: 'I will roar you as gently as any sucking dove; I will roar you as 'twere any nightingale'.

GETTING THE NEEDLE

Acupuncture is the latest craze for American pet owners, following the vogue for animal psychiatry a few years ago. One notable patient was former US Secretary of State Henry Kissinger's arthritic Labrador, Tyler, who was treated by an acupuncturist to ease his dying days.

And in California, a Chinese acupuncture expert used a traditional method to treat stress among goldfish. She inserted needles just below the dorsal fin and is now said to have an aquarium full of relaxed goldfish. Acupuncture is also being used to rid African grey parrots and cockatoos of their nervous habit of relieving boredom by picking at their feathers.

CHEAP AT THE PRICE?

A young man in a remote Kenyan village was ordered to hand over a bull, a ram and two billy goats as a punishment for having made love to all the women in his father-in-law's household. The understandably outraged father-in-law had demanded that the young Casanova should be castrated, but the village elders settled for this less drastic punishment.